Scars
Of A Soldier
Vernon Heppe's
True Story

ADDITIONAL COPIES
of this book may be obtained
directly from Deerfield Publishing
for $10 plus $1 for postage.
Send your order to:

Deerfield Publishing Co.
Box 146
Morley, MI 49336-0146

Library of Congress Catalog Card Number: 94-093873
Copyright © 1994 by Gordon L. Galloway
All rights reserved
Printed in
The United States of America
Published by Deerfield Publishing Company
1613 130th Avenue
Morley, MI 49336
ISBN 0-9644077-0-1

Vernon's story is told in his own words. It is based on interviews, his journal and letters he wrote home to his family during the war. Perhaps one would first like to read Chapter IV, the Kwajalein Battle. It begins on page 68, and I think it will form a natural curiosity about Vernon and his transition from a naive farm boy to a seasoned combat soldier. The battle for Leyte and Okinawa seem even more difficult than Kwajalein, and present interesting reading in later chapters.

This book is dedicated to the memory of Vernon's parents, Elizabeth and Henry Heppe. It is also dedicated to Fred Towersey, in memory of a good friend who was a common link in our lives.

With deep appreciation, I wish to thank my wife, Mary Ann, for her encouragement and the many hours she spent typing the manuscript.

Contents

Portrait Of A Boy
October 1933

Before he was old enough for a gun he would trail behind Grandpa Schramm while he hunted. Grandpa liked to have someone along to carry his game. Vernon had been repeatedly warned never to walk in front of Grandpa, because he always kept both hammers on the old double barrel cocked all the time.

Things were different now. He was 13 years old, finished with school and working full time for his dad on the farm. Not only had Vernon graduated from the eighth grade, he also had two years of experience with the double barrel twenty gauge shotgun. Several rabbits had fallen before his gun, but so far he had been unable to bag a pheasant. Maybe when he could start hitting pheasants his dad would let him go duck hunting with the rest of the men.

It was a cool October day, but the late afternoon sun illuminated the scattered clouds and felt warm. The cornfield was dotted with the cone-shaped stacks of shocked corn and the boy thought that it would be a perfect day to go after the pheasants. He would have an hour or so to hunt before the cows would have to be milked.

The year-old springer spaniel had been following Vernon through his farm chores all day, but a new spirit of excitement tingled in his body when Vernon stepped out of the house with the shotgun and a pocket full of shells.

Vernon's uncle raised purebred springer spaniels, but this dog, Jake, had what they called a watch eye. One eye was real light-colored, almost white, while the other was normal. The eye color difference was easy to spot and made it difficult to sell the dog, so the uncle gave him to Vernon. What a fine hunting dog he was becoming, maybe even the best of the litter. Jake loved to hunt and his tail never seemed to stop wagging. He raced forward then back again, as if to hurry the boy towards the hunt.

Over on Uncle George's place was where the pheasants felt secure. A big old swamp pasture provided plenty of cover for them, and that's where they always headed if they were flushed from a fence row. They even roosted in there at night.

Jake knew there were pheasants at hand. He had an excellent nose and had picked up their scent long before he entered the tall golden rods on the edge of the swamp. Vernon would occasionally get a glimpse of the dog, and could tell that Jake was hot on the trail of something. The dog wasn't moving fast, but could easily be heard sniffing out the trail. All of a sudden there was a flutter of wings, and a large rooster was airborne directly ahead of Vernon. The boy raised the shotgun, fired, and the pheasant seemed to stop in mid-air. The bird went down in the tall grass and Vernon tried to mark the spot in his mind. He tramped around the area looking for the downed bird. Finally, he heard a rustle in the grass ahead, and there stood Jake as proud as could be. Their first pheasant was protruding from both sides of his mouth.

Dad and I on the left with our dog Jake. Grandpa Schramm on the far right, brother Harvey between the tracks. Man in center unknown.
Below: Mother and Dad with me the day I left for the Army.

The Good Old Days

I guess I was brought up in what people now refer to as the good old days. Time probably lets them forget how hard those days were. Not many living conveniences, very little money or good paying jobs and no government to look after you when you were having trouble surviving. Most likely what people miss was the togetherness that existed among families and neighbors. We all had to work with each other to make ends meet and there was usually some type of family or neighborhood activity taking place on weekends for entertainment. Being together so much, the neighborhood became an extension of the family and therefore people felt close to one another, which may not be the case much today.

When I grew up, as hard as times seemed, the old folks thought that we probably had it pretty easy compared to how it had been for them. Grandma and Grandpa Heppe, my Dad's folks, spent six difficult weeks on a sailing ship coming over from Germany. My uncle was only two years old at the time. After Grandma died, Grandpa lived with us for awhile and wanted to talk about all those old times. I was at the age when I didn't care about listening, but now I wish that I had. I don't remember all the details about how they got to Illinois and started farming, but I do remember Grandpa telling how poor they had been in Germany. He said that he and his brother used to throw rocks at the passing trains and the engine fireman would defend himself with chunks of coal. The brothers would then pick up the coal and use it for heat. Seemed like kind of a dangerous system to me. He said that in addition to the coal, they would also go out and steal limbs from the merchant's trees. That would give them enough fuel to keep a little warmer through the winter.

Grandpa Schramm, my mother's father, also was an interesting old fellow. Born in Germany, at the age of sixteen his folks sent him to Paris to learn the cabinet makers trade. When he finished his training, he avoided the mandatory German military tour by signing on to a merchant ship heading to America. It was supposed to be a round trip commitment, but somewhere around Louisiana he jumped ship and took up residence in this country. He ended up in Collom, Illinois and worked as a carpenter, building houses. I guess he did some farming too, but there again I don't remember all the details about how his life got started. I do remember people in the family tellin' that Grandpa could play a horn real good, and had at one time played in John Phillip Sousa's band. I also know that Grandpa was an excellent wood craftsman. Before he moved to Michigan he constructed a clock replica of a cathedral in Paris, and had it shipped up to the farm. It arrived in perfect condition, thanks to a box he had made especially for it. He also made a beautiful jewelry box for my Grandma. It had a lot of different kinds of wood inlaid on the outside of the cover and a miniature design of the outside set inside the box.

Dad's brother, George, was the first of the family to move from Illinois to Michigan, and he sent word back that land was cheap here. My Dad had returned from spending two years in the Army during World War I, and was living with Grandpa and Grandma Heppe in Emmington, Illinois. The Heppes didn't know anything except farming, and the chance to buy cheaper land seemed like a good opportunity, and enough reason to leave Illinois.

My Dad loaded a couple of horses, a cow and as much of his machinery as he could in a train cattle car and headed to Michigan. There was a railroad siding not too far north of here where he unloaded. Someway, either on his own or through George, he purchased forty acres to start his own farm. It wasn't long after that when Grandpa Heppe and other families from Illinois moved up here to settle. The word about cheaper land spread rapidly, but at that time people didn't realize that this cheaper land wasn't going to produce as much as the land in Illinois or that the growing season here was much shorter. Nevertheless they came, and with the Heppes came the Schramm family from Collom, Illinois.

Dad worked for George some while he was getting started, and eventually he got acquainted with the Schramm family and their nineteen-year-old daughter, Elizabeth. They lived not too far from the railroad tracks, and word has it that Mom and Dad would meet on those rail tracks and eventually that courtship would lead to marriage in Nineteen Nineteen.

In Nineteen Twenty I came along, and was the only kid for about six years. It was great being the only kid as I got all of Mom and Dad's attention. I'm sure that those years getting started were a lot of hard work for them, but Mom's time for me would be a lot less as more kids arrived. I can still remember being snuggled between them in the old horse drawn sleigh as we headed out on Saturday night. To keep warm everybody covered themselves with big horse blankets, and Mom was bound and determined that my head was going to be covered, and I was just as determined to have my head out, so I could see things. The blankets were heavy and near impossible to fight off.

Our farm was on Meade Road about seven miles north of Ionia. Mom and Dad moved into the old house that was already there, and aside from minor repairs the house was pretty much the same until Thirty Nine, when Dad made some major improvements. The windows were poor, and there was no insulation, just the wood siding on the outside. It sure would get cold in there if the wood fire went out overnight. A pan of water on the top of the stove would have ice in it come morning. Usually the folks would have a fire going when they got us kids up in the morning, so we'd race down to see who could first get the warm spot behind the stove next to the wall. It's a wonder the place didn't burn down because they would let that stove heat up until the stove pipe was almost red before they would start closing the damper and draft to slow the fire.

We got our water from an old hand pump located in the kitchen by the sink. Our bathroom was a two-holer outhouse, and I tell you the seats were cold enough that you didn't spend much time in there. Toilet tissue was supplied by an outdated Montgomery Ward Catalog.

Mom had a big old wood stove in the kitchen where she did all her cooking. Boy, she was a good cook. I can remember her special treat on Sunday morning was oatmeal with raisins in it.

Both Mom and Dad came from pretty big families. Dad had three brothers and two sisters, Mom had one sister and four brothers. With that background it wasn't any surprise when our family finally started to increase. Harvey was born in Twenty Six followed in three years by Robert, then Katherine and finally Mildred in Thirty Four. We were all born at home. Grandma would come and watch over the delivery and, until Mom was up and around, she would supervise the household.

As the family was getting larger I was entering upon some new experiences in life, starting with school. It was about a mile walk to the Hall School. All eight grades were taught there by just one teacher. Twenty to thirty kids in one room was a lot of responsibility for just one teacher. She also tended the wood fire, performed janitorial duties and was nurse when necessary. During my eight years I had four different teachers. Most were young and got married and left after a couple years.

I liked school and did pretty well. I only got one lickin', but it was a good one. Some older boys were throwing bread crumbs at me and the teacher heard me swear at them. She grabbed a boot and paddled the hell out of me with it. It really hurt.

The bigger kids got to be picking on me more all the time, and one day it came to a head when they grabbed me and threatened to take my pants down in front of the girls. That was about as bad a threat as there could be, and I was really strugglin', crying and biting my lip all at the same time. I got an arm free to swing and caught one of the kids in the guts. He doubled up and started crying. Somebody said, "Let him loose if that's the way he's gonna be." Well getting let loose was about as good a thing as I could think of, but I was also aware that I had the capability to hurt them too. Within a couple of years the situation changed considerably. I discovered I could handle myself pretty well, and instead of being picked on, I was the one picking on the other kids. One year I got a set of leather winter gloves and, imagining myself a boxer, I started punching the other kids a lot. Some told their fathers, who waited and tried to catch me doing it on the way home from school. I was a pretty fast runner though, and they never did get a hand on me. When my brother Harvey started school I got him involved in fighting too, and I'd stand guard so none of the big kids would hurt him.

My responsibilities on the farm increased as I got older. To begin with I was responsible for bringing the cows in from the pasture for milking in the early morning. I still remember being barefoot and running after the cows when the grass was cold and wet from the morning dew. At about eight years I was milking the cows, and shortly after that Dad let me drive the horses. I thought that was a big deal until Dad had me working the horses in the field all the time, and then it wasn't such a big deal.

The first time I worked the horses by myself Dad had three of them hooked to a drag in the middle of a field. Everything went pretty well until somehow I got the drag turned upside down. There was nothing I could do. I couldn't turn the drag right side up, and I didn't dare to let go of the horses for fear they would run away. As there was no one within shouting range to help, I just had to stand there holding them until Dad finally came back.

Usually we only worked two horses together and Dad eventually got me doing the plowing. One horse would travel where the one-bottom plow had gone before and the other walked on the unplowed side. Plowing turned out to be slow and monotonous work. Just walking around that field behind the horses you knew when you started in the morning what would be done at noon, as they moved pretty slow.

Along with all the work, I did have some good times with Dad hunting, fishing and trapping. Though I really didn't care for fishing that much, because Dad wanted me to row the boat while he fished. That wasn't something I enjoyed, so I kinda missed some of the fishing trips. By the time I was eleven he did have a double barrel twenty gauge shotgun for me to hunt with, and it wasn't too long before I started bringing in game for the family meals. There were lots of pheasants and rabbits, but only once did I see a deer track in those years.

Trapping provided extra income for both Dad and myself as muskrat hides were worth almost a dollar-and-a-half apiece. Even skunks were worth some good money, if they didn't have the white stripe down the back. The trouble was that more than once I got watered by a skunk caught in a trap, and then my clothes and I were not real welcome in the house.

The bigger our family got, the more work there was for everyone. I could milk cows pretty fast and Harvey and Robert were big enough to do some work too, so Dad increased our cow herd to bring in more cash. In the winter when the snow was deep, Dad and I would load our milk cans on a sled and push it out to M-66, where Dunsmore's Dairy would pick them up. The most they would take from us was twenty gallons and the rest we separated at home and sold the cream to the creamery in Ionia. There wasn't much money in the cream, maybe five dollars a week.

Of course the more kids that came along, the greater Mom's work load became. Because we did a lot of physical work she had to provide three big meals each day. Some kind of potatoes was the main dish at each meal, usually boiled at night and the leftovers fried in the morning. We ate lots of eggs, usually a couple of meals each day. If we would have been vulnerable to the egg cholesterol we would all have been dead by twenty five. Mom lived to seventy nine and Dad until he was eighty six, so I guess they didn't hurt us.

We always had a big garden and Mom canned lots of vegetables. Of course everybody raised lots of potatoes. They even had what they called a potato vacation when they let the kids out of school to help harvest the potatoes. As I recall we got a nickel a bushel for picking up potatoes. Sure was hard on the old back though, even for a young kid.

People didn't eat as much meat as they do now, probably because there wasn't much money, and the animals could be sold for cash rather than butchering them to eat. We also didn't have a refrigerator to keep meat or dairy products from spoiling. It was a lot of work to preserve the meat once it was cut up. Grandma Heppe would usually come over to help Mother and it would take a couple of days for them to take care of a big hog. They would cook the pork and render out the lard. The meat would be packed in big clay crocks and covered with the grease to seal out the air. A wooden lid would fit snugly on the crock, and the meat kept just fine in the basement until we needed it. They handled beef differently. It too was cooked, but then canned like the vegetables.

Even though we didn't have a refigerator we did have ice when we needed it, especially in the summer when we wanted to make ice cream. George, Dad's brother, had an ice house, and so did a neighbor, Guy Hoppough. Dad would help them cut ice out of Woodard Lake in the winter, and then we'd get a share when we needed it. They would put it in the ice house then pack lots of sawdust around it. Hard to believe, but it would all be intact, even as late as August.

Going to town was a big deal in those days. In the summer Dad would have the old Model T Ford off the jacks and we'd use that. Orleans was the closest town, and was a pretty busy place. They had a grain elevator there where we sold our crops. They even took in beans and hired women to sort them in the winter. Also there was a cheese factory, potato storage and a post office. The Chesapeake & Ohio Railroad went through Orleans and that's what made it a prosperous community.

On Saturday nights in both Orleans and Palo there were free movies. To attract business the local merchants would rent the films and project them on some town building. The people would either sit on the grass or in their autos to watch the movies, and when the film broke occasionally, everybody would toot their horns, flash their lights and hoot and holler until they had it taped back together.

Ionia was the big city then. We sold chickens and eggs down at Curtis's store, and delivered our cream once a week to the creamery where it was processed into butter. Going to Ionia on Saturday was an important social occasion too, because after shopping Mother could get together for a visit with other farmer's wives, plus her folks lived in town. Dad would hit the card room.

The card room was not an exciting place for a kid to hang around. Just a bunch of men sitting around in a smoke-filled room playin' a poker type card game called deuces wild. Each player would get several tokens from the establishment for twenty five cents and use those for chips. The chips could only be spent there for food or pop. Booze wasn't legal then. The only reason I hung around there at all, was because Dad would occasionally give me a nickel for a candy bar.

Dad's other summer fun was playing baseball. It was a small unofficial local league that he played in, and occasionally when they were short a man they would let me in the lineup. Guess I was about twelve then, and my ball playing experience came from that old one-room country school. We'd play other country schools and were pretty good except we never could beat the Hubble School. A bunch of the Johnson boys went there and they were big and good. All the kids played in these games, even the girls, which usually made an out.

I'd always heard my Dad was a pretty good boxer. Even though he wasn't as tall as his brothers, he grew up learning to hold his own with them and he was handy with his fists. I got to witness this first hand at one of the ball games with Lyons, another community east of Ionia. What happened was that Dad was running for a base and this guy tagged him out and at the same time pushed him down. The umpire said, "You're out." Dad got up and started walking toward the guy that tagged him. The umpire said, "I said you're out, get off the field." "I just want to walk over to the guy that pushed me down and talk to him," said Dad. As Dad walked over there the guy stuck out his hand as if to shake, then he took a swing at Dad. That was enough to set Dad off and a big fight took place. I don't remember if there was a winner before the fight broke up, but it was obvious Dad could handle himself.

During the winter, on Saturday night when the chores were done, Mom and Dad would pack us in the sleigh for a trip to some neighbor's house. We had a deluxe sleigh in those days. It had a windshield, and below a slot for the reins to go through up to the horses. A roof kept the snow off our heads but there were no side curtains so it still could get mighty cold. At someone's house all the neighbors would collect for the Pedro card games. Along with the Heppes and Schramms were the Eckerts, McPhersons, Petersons, Nelsons and the Haysmers. A little hard cider from Nelson Haysmer's cider mill usually was brought along and I can remember some of the big folks got pretty silly from its effect. We kids were usually asleep in some part of the house before the card games were over and we headed home.

It was kinda rough going to school during the bad winter weather. There never was any transportation other than our feet to go that mile. School started at nine o'clock but our day started much earlier. First the cows had to be milked and I had to check my trap line. The same work was waiting after school, so we were ready to go to bed at night. We still had fun at school though, as there was a good ice skating pond nearby where we spent our noon hours. All we had was old clamp-on skates which came off a lot, but I still was a pretty good skater. There was one mishap when I skated into some shallow ice and went flying as it broke through. I cut my chin good on the broken ice, and it bled a lot. I still carry that scar.

The kids in our family got along with each other, except the girls fought a lot. Mildred liked to scratch, but the folks brought that to a halt when they threatened to cut off her nails if she didn't stop. They had a reputation of following through on their threats without issuing second chances, so we listened the first time. I only remember getting one big licking from Mom. I wanted to go with Dad some place, and she said no. As he left in the car I started to chase after him. Ma grabbed her strap off the nail by the chimney and kinda lost control. Boy, she could hit hard. My legs had black and blue marks for some time after that.

About once a week Harvey, Robert and I would walk down and visit Ronnie Parmeter. He was probably in his fifties and had grown up around that area. Ronnie was married and did a little farming on his forty acres, but didn't have much and was barely scraping by. He was the type of guy that kids liked to be with. He always had lots of stories about old times and Indians. Once when he was in school a couple Indians peeked in the school window and the teacher told the kids to lie on the floor while she locked the door. Ronnie also had a cigar box full of rattlesnake tails that he had accumulated from his farm. When I was older, I helped him harvest his hay and you always had to watch out forkin' the hay as a rattler might be laying out sunning himself. You'd occasionally even find them on the scaffolding in the barn.

Sometimes we stayed a little late at Ronnie's and it was dark when we headed back home. To tease Robert, Harvey and I would take off running ahead of him. He was scared but didn't cry or anything, just ran like hell tryin' to keep up with us. He always said that's what made him a good runner, just running after us.

We did play a mean trick on Ronnie's bulldog one day. Ronnie had to walk past our place down to the corner to get his mail. His dog would always take a little side trip over to our barn and lap up the milk out of the cat's dish. One day when he came in we shut the door behind him. We grabbed him and roughed up his behind with a corn-cob and then spread turpentine over the raw area. Boy, that dog tore through the barn door and never did come back. Ronnie hadn't missed his dog, but later we heard him telling somebody, "I don't know what got into that dog. He ran right by me headed for home, didn't even stop when I called him."

We pulled some other tricks, too. For the horse we wound an ear of corn in the electric fence. He got a couple of jolts trying to eat it, then finally left it alone. Our dog also fell victim to our meanness when we set his metal feed dish on a rubber inner tube and wired it up to the electric fence, too.

One day we kinda got paid back for some of our meanness, and it was a real scary time. I had brought the horses up from the field as I could see a big storm brewin' in the west. About the time I got in our yard a big lightning bolt hit behind the house and the horses jumped around a lot. As I was putting them away in the barn, Harvey came running up yellin' that Robert had been hit by lightning. I ran up to the house with Harvey and found Mother leaning over Robert who was knocked out on the ground. He had been pushing the lawn mower by the old tree, when the bolt hit the tree. The steel U bolts holding the mower handle together must have been against Robert's chest as he had two burn marks on his chest and his undershirt had started to burn. Also he was burned where the metal buttons from his overalls touched his body, and there were pieces of bark from the tree stuck in his neck. Dad wasn't home so Mom told me to hurry down to Raymond Hoppoughs for help. I jumped on my bike for Hoppoughs, and they said later that when they saw me coming down the road they knew something was wrong as they'd never seen anyone ride one that fast. Raymond brought his car down to take Mother and Robert to the doctor. Robert was still unconscious and stiffened right up when Mother carried him upstairs to Dr. Marsh's office. I don't know what Dr. Marsh did, but Robert finally came to and they asked him how he felt. He said it felt as though a big stone had hit him. Everybody thought that from then on Robert would always be scared of lightning, but that wasn't the case. When a bad storm went through everybody else would be up fretting while Robert slept right through it.

When I graduated from the eighth grade I was thirteen and there was little talk of me going to high school. Mom had only gone through the eighth grade and Dad only the fourth. There were no buses then, and unless you were willing to walk the seven miles back and forth each day, you didn't go. I was a pretty capable farm worker by that time and Dad needed my help too. He had remodeled the barn and we were milking about twelve cows, and I could also do about any kind of field work with the horses.

In those days if you didn't have your horses out in the field to work by seven o'clock you weren't a very good farmer. You and the horses got an hour rest at noon, and then you were back out until five and it was time to milk the cows again. At harvest time the neighbors all traded work. To keep things even, if your neighbor raised more acres of a crop than you did, then he would furnish more men to help harvest your crop. No money changed hands and for the most part everyone worked well together. It was hard work though. The corn was all cut by hand, then tied into bundles, and shocked together to dry in the field. In October or later, the shocks were tipped onto a wagon and hauled to the shredder which removed the ears of corn and blew the stalks into the barn for winter feed. The wheat and other grain was also bundled up and then run through a threshing machine. The straw was blown out into a stack, and we had to carry the ninety pound bags of grain up the barn hill and dump them in the granary.

When I wasn't doing farm work I tried to pick up extra jobs. In those depression years there weren't many jobs. I did pick apples pretty regular for a couple weeks in the fall each year. You could earn sixty cents an hour, and some of the guys in the factory were only earning forty cents. For a couple of winters Dad and I both worked sorting potatoes for a guy who hauled them to Kentucky to sell, returning with a load of coal.

One winter Harvey and I cut wood for neighbors. We got eighty cents a cord to cut, split and pile it in their woods. It all was cut by hand using a crosscut saw and when we produced four cords a day I thought we were doing well. I was so sore I could hardly move at night. Eventually we toughened up, because we got up to five cords and on one good day finished six.

In the winter I still trapped, and the older I got the more skilled I was at bringing in the muskrats. I had developed a new technique for getting them which was slightly illegal, but was quite efficient. The way it worked was that when there was a thin coat of ice on a pond I'd locate a muskrat house and the runways coming out of it. Old Jake my all-purpose hunting dog would pounce on the house and I'd wait for the rats to head out of it down a runway. They were easy to spot from the bubbles they would release as they swam along. They kept their head against the ice so a shot from the old twenty two stunned them good until I got them out. Sometimes you could get five or so from one house.

One morning Jake and I had just headed out for this pond and some muskrats, when I saw Louie Kahl go by in his green Thirty Nine Chevy. Louie was the local game warden and I didn't think too much about it at the time. Jake and I got started on the morning hunt and I missed a rat on my first shot. This was fortunate because shortly thereafter Louie appeared on the other side of the pond and yelled out, "What ya doin'?" "I'm just rabbit hunting," I replied. "I think you're hunting muskrats illegally with that gun, and it's out of season too." "No sir, I'm just rabbit hunting." Of course while we were talkin' old Jake is over there pouncing on the rat house. "Jake, get over here!" Jake looked at me as if to say, "No let's get some more muskrats." "I'll just look around here for a little bit." Louie poked around my coat to see if I had a rat hidden in it, then said, "If I find anything I'll get in touch with you." "I think I'm gonna hunt some place else." I said. I was hoping he wouldn't find a dead rat laying around and blame it on me, or worse yet, show up at the farm and look in the barn where thirty rats were hanging. I left the pond and headed home, but Louie never showed up there. He knew Dad pretty well, and was probably satisfied with scaring me, which he had.

Dad talked me into getting into the livestock business, so with my extra money earned from trapping and picking apples I bought a calf.

It wasn't long after that though, that my grandpa died and I had to sell my calf and buy a suit of clothes for his funeral. That soured me on the livestock business.

At fourteen, Dad rewarded my work efforts by presenting me with an old Model T Ford truck that he had bought for twenty five dollars. He said, "Boy, it's yours. If you wreck it, it's still yours." I was really proud of that old truck. I didn't use it much in the winter because it was hard to start. In the summer it gave me new freedom to move out. We fixed a platform for the back so I could haul our milk all the way to town now. I had no license for me, or the truck. There was no insurance either. It didn't use much gas. The tank was under the seat, so before we headed over to Woodard Lake swimming, we'd stick a measuring stick down in the tank to see if we had enough gas to get back and forth.

By Nineteen Thirty Nine Dad had purchased an International H tractor. That was a tractor that did some real work. Years before he and George had purchased an old Fordson, but it required more work cranking it to start than you ever accomplished in the field. With the new tractor Dad required me less on the farm, especially since Harvey and Robert were doing more work. I still helped with the milking though, as I was real fast. I could milk eight cows in forty minutes. Robert dumped the milk for me and I just moved on to the next cow. The cows knew I was fast and would let their milk right down. I didn't want anyone else to milk them either, as they were used to my speed and someone slower might change their habits.

That summer I worked in construction helping to build houses and barns in the local area. With the extra income and what I had saved for a long time, I bought a Twenty Nine Chevrolet for a hundred dollars. I removed the right front seat and built a platform in the back so I could haul three cans of milk. We were now hauling milk to both Dunsmore and Yeomans Dairy, and making pretty good money.

The Model T now became my race car. There wasn't much money for frills or for that matter even to keep it running. When the tires got worn down they occasionally would blow, and with no money to buy new ones we developed a cheap fix. We'd pack them with oats and water. The oats would swell and sprout giving the tire good pressure.

Times were getting better now. It had been hard for all of us. Mother had made our underwear and the girl's dresses out of patterned chicken feed bags. We had patches upon patches on our britches, and our sock holes were darned so much they were uncomfortable. We had enough to eat though, and seemed like a happy family. With the war years coming on, there were more jobs and people were getting more money for their produce. Dad remodeled the house, fixing four bedrooms upstairs, running water inside and insulation on the outside.

I progressed from my Chevrolet to a Thirty Six Ford, which I didn't use to haul milk. In the spring of Forty Two I went to work at the Reed factory and bought a top of the line Thirty Nine Chevrolet. It had hydraulic brakes, a heater and defroster. I even had insurance on it. I also had money and the time to have some fun and meet some girls. Before that I barely had money enough for myself, let alone payin' for two.

I had some good buddies that also worked at the factory, Donald Minikey, Jerry Selleck and Raymond Wagner. We really enjoyed life with money to spend and good transportation. We hit the movies, played softball on Sundays and went to Reeds Lake near Grand Rapids to ride the roller coaster. We were also in regular attendance at the roller skating rink at Long Lake. Even though I was getting out more now, I still was pretty much a country kid and not too concerned about what was going on in the rest of the world. I registered for the draft like the rest of my friends, and was classified 1A. I guess I figured I might be called up, but then again the war might be over before they got to me.

They finally drafted me in the fall of Forty Two. I was not the only one to get his draft notice, and it didn't seem that big a deal. We had to go take a test for the Army and I passed that with a hundred percent. They sent us home for a couple weeks before we left for training. During that time we got a little wilder driving our cars. Guess we felt like having a last fling before we had to go. Once we got up to eighty miles per hour racing on East Main Street in Ionia. It's a good thing no one stepped out, otherwise we'd have hit them. The law wasn't as quick then as now.

When the time came for me to leave for the Army, family and friends saw me off at the rail station. There were no tears, I guess everyone just expected it was going to happen. If I'd known what I was getting into, there would have been a big puddle of tears, mine.

It was on the Fourteenth of November, seven days past my twenty second birthday, that I got on that Saturday noon train in Ionia. I never knew the train would go so far before it brought me home again, as it would be August Sixteenth Nineteen Forty Five before I returned.

Soldier Boy

The train arrived at Fort Custer Michigan around nine o'clock that night, and you should have seen the fine supper they set up for us. I thought it was real nice of them to do that, but about two days later I found out how it was done, because I was doing it. Kitchen patrol, or KP they call it here. Boy, what a day that was. Up at four thirty in the morning and work until ten thirty at night, with no time off. Most of the time, just to look busy, I was carrying coffee and water pitchers back and forth across the room. A friend suggested we stop and have a pop. A KP pusher saw us before we got the pop, and had us unload a truck full of potatoes. When I got those pitchers back in my hands, they stayed there the rest of the day.

I got my shots and clothes the first day there. My pants were too long so I had to wait and have them shortened. A Private First Class (PFC) told me to wait outside when my pants were done. I waited, but he was nowhere in sight. I knew where to go so I returned to my barracks. Well, that was my first big mistake in the Army, as you are not supposed to know where you have been, or where you are going unless someone tells you. I was told never to forget that, not even once.

November 18, 1942

"Dear family,"

"We had lots of fun coming here on the train, and I'm having a very good time down here. There are eighty men in my group and they have furnished us with all the clothes we need, even underwear and shaving things. We are in quarantine for awhile, and just stay inside with nothing much to do. The shots weren't too bad, but before we got them some of the guys here said they had two inch needles with hooks on them. We told the new guys that came in after us the same thing, so guess we're just as bad."

"The meals are good with lots of sugar and ice cream, but no butter, and that is hell."

"I will not have to get married now, because I know how to make a bed."

"I am sending my other clothes home, because they say we don't need them anymore. I hope Dad gets a deer up north, so that if I get home next weekend I can see him."

> your Soldier Boy,
> Vernon

We started training at Camp Custer, but it looked more to me like a bunch of guys running around in a circle. This mean sergeant stood up on a platform yelling at us to go fast, and occasionally he would get down and poke someone in the ass to make them go faster. He looked just like the mean sergeant I saw in a show about a month before I came into the Army.

Well I didn't have to worry about getting home for a weekend off, because the day before we left I had KP again. It was up again at four thirty, dishin' out food, washing dishes and mopping floors. I think the floors were cleaner than the dishes. Those sarges were really tough. They didn't let you sit down at all.

November 20, 1942

"I am on the train and in bed while I write this. The major in charge will not tell us where we are going, but I sure like this trip. Boy, it's all right. We stopped in Chicago to get on a train with pullman cars, and a dining car too."

November 22, 1942

"Since we left Michigan we've been off this train once, for 30 minutes in Iowa. Every time we come up on a tunnel someone yells, 'tunnel!', and we close the windows. Otherwise, the car fills with smoke."

"South Dakota sure is hilly, and the houses are real far apart. Wyoming looks like poor country. Montana has lots of mountains and snow, and is it ever cold there. We've sure had a lot of fun on the train, but we didn't get off for two whole days. We have all we want to eat and just sleep and look out at the countryside. There are twelve carloads of us. Some boys are homesick, but not me. I think it's a lot of fun. They have a porter on each car that makes beds and cleans the car. Harold from Ionia is with me."

Our train went through Spokane, Washington and then down into Oregon. They still wouldn't tell us where we were going. I think they confused us more than they did the enemy.

November 24, 1942

"After 97 hours on the train we arrived at Camp Adair in Oregon. We came through Portland to get here, and are 30 miles from the sea coast. Camp Adair is a new camp, and it is sure wet here. Harold is in the next bed, but tomorrow we move to our regular barracks. There are lots of officers here and good eats. Tell me all the news so I will have something to read. Seems like I have been gone a month, but there's a lot going on and a lot to learn."

November 29, 1942

"It sure is a different Army today than it was yesterday. I had to carry an 85 pound barracks bag for a mile. Not so bad for a tough farm kid, but for others it was a problem."

"I don't know which outfit I'm in. I asked the captain and he said to ask the squad leader. There are only three of us left in the barracks today, I'm waiting here for someone to tell me what to do."

"I couldn't write sooner. We were ordered not to."

"Please send some wire coat hangers. We have none to hang up our clothes."

"They say we will have no weekends off for quite awhile. Everyday seems the same."

Some of the boys had already been there a couple of weeks before we arrived, and knew how to march. We didn't do that well. When the Sergeant gave, "to the rear march," we didn't do it right, so he had me and another boy fall out after supper, and he gave us two full hours of to the rear march. Boy, after that I could really do it good.

This Army life could really get to you sometimes. We started drilling at six in the morning, and had to train in the mud all day until five. We then had to fall back in wearing a class A uniform for retreat at five thirty. We all had double bunks so you can imagine everyone trying to change their clothes at the same time. What a life. It looked better in a book than being here, just ask me.

The food wasn't too bad if you liked it, cause whatever was left from one day you got the next, or maybe even the day after that, until it was gone. We always ate breakfast at the same time, so whether the meal was good or bad depended on when the cooks got up. The bacon might only be warm if they got up late or it might be so crisp it wouldn't stay on your fork if they got up early. They must have had a lot of carrots, for in one meal I saw them fixed three different ways. They didn't cut up the chicken, they hacked it up with a cleaver, so you could eat the bones I guess.

I spent Thanksgiving on KP, and never washed so many pots and pans. Every time I'd get one washed the cook would dirty another. I did get a good meal and ate about ten pieces of pie, but it wasn't a good day.

November 29, 1942

"I am all right so far, so don't worry about me because I will be fine here. I am not sick or homesick. I think of home a lot and wonder what you are doing. The only time I feel bad is when I write home or something, but I'm getting along good."

"Not much time to think, so much to do. We're up at six and to bed by eleven. We drill eight until twelve, then one until five. On Saturday we work for four hours. When I can, I go to the show or post exchange (PX)."

"Camp Adair contains 50,000 acres and a lot of good men, and officers too. A lot of boys from the South are here and they sure talk slow. In our latrine there are several stools in a row with no partitions. I was waiting in line and talking to another guy, when one of the stools became available. From the back of the line this southern boy said, 'You fixin' to use that hole?' That was the first time I ever heard anyone fixin' to do anything."

"I'm going to be a rifleman in an infantry squad, but I don't have a gun yet. Soon I will get a 30 cal M-1. Its clip holds eight shells and is automatic, so all you have to do is pull the trigger and it keeps shooting. I wish I had a shotgun here because there's lots of pheasants and rabbits. Did Dad get a deer? Is Harvey trapping for muskrats?"

"Yes, I try to go to church every Sunday, and no, I don't need any money. Harold is in a barracks two blocks away. Here's a list of things I do need. Six boxes of cough drops, coat hangers, hair oil, regular razor blades and shaving lotion."

The drill sergeants at Adair were really mean. Most had been in the service for twenty five to thirty years and were weekend alcoholics. They had never seen any fighting and wouldn't go overseas with us. That was probably a good thing for them because one of our boys might have shot them, as they were so mad at them. They did everything possible to make our lives miserable and show us the Army was boss. Last week our sergeant asked for volunteers to be truck drivers. Dad had been in the Army during World War I, and he told me never to volunteer for anything. When the truck driving volunteers came back we found out they had been pushing wheelbarrows all day. The sergeant explained afterwards that he hadn't meant they were going to become truck drivers.

I learned the hard way about raising my hand when we first got to Adair. We had been out on a long march and I really had sore feet. The sergeant asked if anyone had blisters, which everyone did. I had one the size of a half dollar. I wasn't smart and raised my hand. He directed us to the dispensary. There they sprayed the blisters with something to freeze them, and took a hooked knife and pulled the skin off. With the skin off they hurt like hell and didn't heal for a month. That cured the whole company from ever having blisters again.

Seems like we spent most of our time getting ready for inspections. Our bunks had to be made all the same and good. Our clothes all had to be folded, and lined up like everybody else. The floors had to be mopped every morning and really good on Saturday. The captain and sergeant would look the barracks all over then we would fall out in the company street and have guns, shoes and haircuts checked. If we all passed this, and we weren't assigned a weekend detail we might get a half day off to go to town.

It was a new camp and real muddy when it rained, and it rained all the time. At one time we went 23 days without seeing Mt. Hood, which wasn't that far away. I guess the government had just recently taken over all this land where the camp sat. There had been nice farms there and the land looked real productive. You could see that a lot of the fields had crops harvested from them that year. There were farm buildings left scattered around, and the land was really rutted up from the Army coming in and building all the barracks.

December 9, 1942

"It hasn't frozen here yet, but it rains a lot. We march in the rain, lay down in the mud and water and have wet feet every day. I have a bad cold and sore feet, but you have to be awfully sick to go to the hospital. Out of 96 divisions there are 1400 men in the hospital now, and six died last Sunday. There are more going in every day. I haven't had any butter for two weeks, and milk is limited. We do have lots of meat and I have gained ten to twelve pounds. The grass is still real green and it is so wet here that there is moss all over the trees."

"We marched 20 miles over a mountain, about six times on the double. Our dinner was in the field. They are sure putting it to us, but I've learned a lot since I've been here."

"It will be 30 days before we can get a weekend pass. Is Dad working yet? Has Harvey caught any rats? I have 30 dollars left and I have 5 dollars going each month for government bonds. Harold and I go to the show a lot."

"One day we were out in the field practicing rifle firing positions without ammunition and the sergeant ordered us to form a firing line in the prone position. My spot had a water puddle so I went down on my toes and elbows and kinda held my body out of the water. The sergeant looked down the line and saw my body up higher than the rest. He said, "Heppe, you're not in the right position." I lowered down a little, but he walked over and put his foot in the middle of my back and pushed my belly down in the cold water. Didn't matter much then, I just laid there and let it soak in."

December 11, 1942

"I'm wondering if you're getting my letters, because I'm not getting your letters here. Did Dad get his job back at the factory? Don't they need men at the factory? If he gets his job back that will be the best news I could get."

"Have you got the corn husked yet? Are the cows giving a good flow of milk? How is Jake doing? Does he look for me? Has Harvey trapped any more muskrats or mink?"

"I'm in the 96th Division, which has a lot of men from Michigan and Illinois. Also there are a lot of southern boys in it. They sure talk funny, but I'm getting used to listening to them."

"I haven't got a rifle yet, but I'm learning a lot about compass and map reading."

"Not much to do on Saturday and Sunday. I go to church every Sunday."

"We walk or run everywhere. I haven't had a ride since I've been here. We had to go through a barbwire entanglement today."

"I haven't had a letter in a long time."

They finally gave us our rifles and made us carry them every place. We were instructed how to take them apart and clean them, but I began to wonder if we would ever get to shoot them. We spent hours and days going through dry fire drills and firing positions. What we did most was walk and double time in the rain and mud. It was impossible to stay dry. When we got some snow they issued us four-buckle overshoes, but here is how we used them. The stones on the road would cut them up so we carried them in our packs while we walked four miles on the road and got our feet good and wet. Then when we left the road we put them on. That really made good Army sense. We had raincoats too, but if they were put on, everyone had to put them on and keep them buttoned, even 45 minutes after the rain stopped. By the time you took them off you were getting wet inside from the heat and sweat. Most of the time you just got soaked and let the air dry you off somewhere during the march.

Trying to keep your uniform clean, with the mud everywhere, was a real chore. We had to fall out in a clean uniform every day. It took four days to get them back from the laundry, so we didn't send them. We just washed them out each day in the shower. The place was really muddy when we got through.

Sometimes they wouldn't give us much notice before we left for the field and everyone would be rushing to pack all the required items. When they said fall out in 30 minutes, that meant they left in 30 minutes. There were usually a few stragglers running to catch up. A lot of times their personal things like razors and socks were falling out if they hadn't packed too good. We went through the packing ritual many times even if we didn't go to the field. A lot of times we would just march a little ways from the barracks and set up our tents. There we would have to lay all our things out in the mud and stand by our tent for inspection. Each man would carry half a tent, so there would always be two of you with extra underwear, socks, shaving items spread out neatly in front of your tent. If you forgot a sock, they could always tell that the sock roll wasn't big enough and that meant a KP detail. When the captain approached your tent you stood in front of it with your rifle at port arms. You were supposed to hold the rifle so that he could easily grab and inspect it. He'd look through the barrel and mechanism for dirt. I always had mine real clean, except once he found dirt behind the plate where the cleaning pad was kept. After inspection we had to roll up all our stuff that had lain in the mud and take it back in to wash for the next inspection.

On Saturday morning they always had a thorough barracks inspection. They checked our beds, personal items, rifles and how clean the barracks were. We thought we had it made for a pass into town one weekend, but the captain brought his white glove along and found dirt on top of the heating duct so we spent our Saturday cleaning some more.

We did finally fire our rifles and did learn a lot of army, but also how much you can miss home. A lot of time was spent digging foxholes. We would dig them in the morning and fill them in at night.

What fun! After you dig the hole you must hide all the dirt that comes out so the hole is not easy to see. This makes it more difficult to fill them in because you've got to get all that dirt back. One time me and another boy did a two-man foxhole and instead of filling it all in at night, we put sticks, leaves and a little dirt over it. The sergeant inspects to make sure they're all filled in and ours looked good. Unfortunately after we lined up and started back to camp the captain drove his jeep into our hole and you can guess what happened. We could hear him hollering, "Who dug this hole?" It was dark and we were on our way back so they never did find out it was ours. If they had, we would have been diggin' a lot of foxholes the next week I bet.

December 22, 1942

"There isn't much of anything to buy here for Christmas presents, so guess you'll have to wait."

"I am a rifleman in the Third Squad, Third Platoon, Third Battalion, 383rd Regiment, 96th Division. So there you have it. I hope you can understand it because it took me a long time. There are about 235 men in a company. A company has three rifle platoons, a heavy weapons platoon, a machine gun platoon and the headquarters staff. Each platoon has three squads."

"We have a day room in our barracks that has games and cards to pass time on the weekends. Our bathrooms have six toilets and six showers with hot and cold running water. I sleep above the cook and I'm good friends with him, so if I want anything extra to eat he will get it for me."

"Boy, my feet are sore on the balls. I have been walking too much. I thought I was tough, but guess I'm not. We are required to walk at least 85 miles a week."

"We got lots of gas mask training this week. They say our gas mask and rifle are our best friends."

"Hope you will overlook all the misspelled words."

"This is my address now.   Pvt Vernon W. Heppe
                              Co I 383rd Inf Rd
                              96th Inf Div
                              SS#36407413"

December 23, 1942

"How are things back home? I should say where you live, as this is my new home and a good home too."

"Sell off my old car and use the money to pay off some of your debts. Don't send money to me as I got more than when I came into the Army."

"I can hear a radio playing upstairs in the barracks."

"How often you get KP and details depends on how good you are and how clean you keep your rifle."

"Tell Harvey and Robert not to shoot all the rabbits. I want to have some when I come home."

December 26, 1942

"We had a swell Christmas dinner."

"They are sending the older boys home, those 44 and older. Guess they can't take it anymore. Company I is one of the toughest. We train more and stay in the field longer than most. They don't give us time to be homesick, but I do see some boys sitting by themselves and they don't say a word. Also I have heard that a couple of guys in another company just couldn't take it and hung themselves."

"I am sorry you haven't caught any muskrats this year Harvey, but you will next year, so don't feel bad."

"Some fellows feel this war will be over soon, but I don't. What do you think?"

December 27, 1942

"I sure was pleased with the long letter from home."

"The red mud around here gets on everything."

"There are two divisions here, the 96th and 104th. The barracks go as far north and south as you can see."

"I ran two miles at double time. Only three of us did, the rest dropped out. I hope the war does not last long. Sounds like it's getting better."

"The Lieutenant brought over a quart of rum for Christmas. It tasted good."

"There are a lot in the hospital. If you get sick they don't give you medicine, just put you in the hospital."

December 29, 1942

"This week we shot our rifles from 300 yards. I got 47 hits out of 50. At 200 yards I had five bulls prone and five kneeling. There was one other company boy that got ten bulls. My rifle sure shot good and the sergeant said it was damn good shooting."

"We did double time from the range to the barracks. There were only twelve men left and I didn't think I would make it, but I thought if the sergeant could take it, so could I. I sure was tired, and so was he."

January 2, 1943

"My shoes had water in them today and my raincoat leaks like hell. Lots of the towns around are flooded."

"They tell us that it is going to be a long war. I hope I see a little of it before I come home, because I would hate to have all this training without using it a little."

"We had a little New Year's Eve party, and our officers came around and the sergeants too."

"The sergeant says if I shoot good enough I may get my private first class (PFC) stripe."

January 5, 1943

"I fired expert today. We had to fire from the sitting, kneeling, and standing position, then go to prone for rapid fire. I shot 201 out of 220. There were only two boys higher in the three platoons. Our platoon was the highest in the company with seven firing expert. My squad was the best with four experts. The lieutenant had promised a carton of cigarettes for the best squad. The sergeant was certainly pleased."

Things were going good enough now that we also had a little fun on the range. Under each target was a pit with a man in it. It was his job to hold a white stick and marker up over the black target where the last shot had hit. The man shooting would know where he shot and how to adjust his gun sights. Sometimes, when the guy held the marker up the shooter would put a hole right through the marker. Then they would call up and want to know who was shootin' on that target. Sometimes when the guy in the pit was warned that the lieutenant was coming up to shoot, he would put his marker up on the opposite side the lieutenant shot. The lieutenant would try to adjust his sights to correct and would end up all confused. Eventually he'd call down and want to know who was marking his target.

January 9, 1943

"I had KP from 5:30 a.m. to 9:00 p.m., then got a class A pass to go into town. I didn't have that good a time."

January 12, 1943

"Sorry to hear Harold Mitchell was killed. Sure hard for the family to get word. Guess the war is not over like some think it is."

"I had ten pancakes for breakfast. We have fifteen minutes to get in the mess hall after we're called, otherwise the doors are locked."

"I'd sure like to be a corporal with $66 a month. That's not hay!"

"We shot from 800 yards today and got 94 hits out of 300. Our platoon was the highest again."

"Today we found out that those in our unit over 38 can get out of the Army if they sign up for a defense job."

"I was mighty pleased with brother Harvey's letter."

"We had bayonet practice today."

January 14, 1943

"Boy do I know how to mop floors now!"

"I have to fall out for sick call about every morning because I have poison oak real bad. They put some red stuff on it which does no good, but makes me look like an Indian. The other fellows get a good laugh out of that. About the only thing that helps is to take a shower and let the GI soap dry on my body."

"We had to parade in front of the colonel and general this week. Our company was judged the best. I really like to march with the music."

"For a test this week we had to go 12 miles in three hours, carry a man our own weight on our back for 75 yards and run 300 yards. I did it all OK and ran the 300 yards in 44

seconds."
January 19, 1943

"We went out overnight and boy was it cold. About ten above zero I think. We left with full field pack and went about ten miles, then set up our tents and dug foxholes. Later we left for a twelve mile night hike and when we finally went to bed I didn't even take my clothes off."

"I went through the bayonet course and got expert. You had to do the course in 40 seconds for expert, and I did it in 32."

"I got a pass and went to Portland over the weekend. I spent $20, two dollars for the bus, eight dollars for the hotel and I bought a new pair of shoes for $4.45. We had a good oyster supper and went to the George White Service Club. Boy, I had a good time. All you wanted to eat free, and dancing and games. We played games with two girls."

"The sergeant said we were in 14 week type training, and we've only been here six weeks. They really are pushing us. We have to have three more weeks before they will send us to combat."
January 22, 1943

"Say, how are the cows doing now? With as many as you've got, how do you find room for them all in the barn? How is the old horse? Is Jake the same as always? I sure would like to see him now. I bet he knows me yet, or doesn't he?"

"I went to sick call again today. Have poison oak on my arms, back and face. The fellows still kid me when I come back with the red stuff on my face."

"We have a parade tonight. Boy, I like them."
January 23, 1943

"I go on sick call every morning now. The poison oak is hard to get rid of. A lot of guys in camp have it as it grows all over the place. We have one hill they've named Poison Oak."

"It isn't supposed to snow here, but it does, and is about two feet deep."

"I haven't been falling out lately because my shoes are bad. The captain says I don't have to go out until they get my new ones in. I do work in the barracks and day room. It's easy."

"Last night I did go out on a six and a half mile hike wearing overshoes. We did one mile of it in the fields and it was snowing real hard. Had to carry full field pack, gas mask and our guns. Only walked 120 steps per minute, which wasn't bad. I had to clean my gun four times because of the snow."

"You asked where my friends here are from. They are from all over, Texas, Louisiana, Illinois, Kansas and Michigan."

"I took out $10,000 worth of US Army insurance. That's the most I could get and costs $6.60 a month."

"The post exchange store has lots of things, beer too, but they sell out fast."

"If I get through this army OK, I would take a lot for it because it has been something new for me, and I guess it is OK."

January 24, 1943

"I hope you are better than I am. I think the doctor here might be OK for horses. I can't get rid of this poison oak. I have it all over my body and the red stuff they put on doesn't work. It itches a lot at night and just about drives me nuts."

"I eat a lot of candy here, I don't know why."

"Say, how would you like to trade places with me. The Army is pretty good at that. How did you like it Dad? Some of the things are kind of foolish, but I guess they know what they are doing."

"All you hear now is about being shipped out. We had to get our barracks bag marked last night and they wouldn't take our clothes at the laundry. Looks kinda funny to me. You hear lots of things and never can tell."

January 28, 1943

"If I got as wet back home as I do here, I'd die. We sit on the ground a lot. It's really cold with lots of snow and we get our feet wet too."

"I got a letter from some Maxine, and wondered who she was. I wrote to a friend's cousin in Kansas and you should see the letter I got back, three sides full. Boy is she a good looking girl. She sent me a picture of herself. I have to send one back."

"Today we had a parade with our bayonets on. The first time for that. We also stand guard duty with our guns loaded. We are real soldiers now, and don't think we aren't."

"My best friend is a fellow named Snyder from Iowa. We are the same size and back each other up. Hang together like two bugs. The platoon lieutenant says that on the long hikes the rest of the guys like to be along just to hear Snyder and me bitch about how hard it is."

"I sent a present home to Katherine (sister). She has to write me now."

January 30, 1943

"We had an inspection by the colonel, captain and lieutenant, and they only found a couple of dirty guns."

"Say how is Jake now that he's getting older? Does he get around much or just lay behind the stove now that it's cold?"

"How many pigs have you got now?"

"Yesterday we had to crawl up a hill and it was raining and snowing at the same time. The ground was snow and mud. Boy, was I cold when I got back to barracks. It's a wonder we all don't get sick and die, but they give us so many shots you couldn't get sick if you wanted to."

"With gas rationed, can you get enough for the tractor? How does it start this winter?"

"The snow is about gone now. We still march in the parades. I sure like to march to music."

"The men over 38 are going home soon. For the last week they have been doing KP and details around camp. That makes it easier for us."

"For your information, there are 45 men in a rifle platoon, three platoons in a rifle company, three rifle companies per battalion, three battalions to a regiment."

"I would like to buy my rifle after the war. They cost $84 now, but might cost more later. I can shoot a man sized target at 800 yards, but it is best at shooting 400 or 500 yards. I got ten bulls in a row at 300 yards. The Japs sure want to get out of the way when we come."

"Boy, I have a lot of friends here, but cannot seem to get in good with the captain. The cook is a hard fellow, but gets me things, lots of oranges and apples."

"The boys shot dice all day yesterday and are at it again this morning. Eight of them are shooting right in front of my bed. I have not played dice or cards while in camp. They are broke a week after payday. I think some of these guys are crooked. One buddy of mine did make $24 yesterday. He sure is lucky."

"We are not supposed to take any pictures in camp now."

"I go to the show a lot as it only costs 15 cents. Seems like all the pictures have something to do with the war. I guess they want to teach us to fight all the time. They sure want to make good soldiers out of us."

"The sergeant asked me to give close order drill out on the road. I never did it before, but did OK, so guess I can do it."

February 2, 1943

"I went to Portland again last weekend, and had a lot of fun. It's about a three hour trip but doesn't cost much and a lot of girls are there at the service club. Corvallis is the closest town to the army post. We go in there quite often and roller skate. Only 35 cents."

"Guess I won't be going to town for awhile as one of our fellows came down with measles and they won't let us go anywhere for ten days."

"I've been acting squad leader for awhile."

February 4, 1943

"Our captain got promoted and we got a new one."

"We've been carrying full pack to the field on a regular basis now. That includes eating utensils, tent and our clothes.''

"They have not been letting us have a fire in the barracks lately, so we live like cave men. It's supposed to toughen us up for being outside in the tents."

February 14, 1943

"Sure was glad to get the letter from Mother and Dad as there was lots of news."

"I've been playing some cards here. The only game they play is for money. The last time I played I had $2.50 more than when I started, so I quit."

'I'm getting fat, weight 202 pounds. I quit eating candy and ice cream."

"Our company was chosen best of the 383rd Regiment."

"I played some football in the mud yesterday. One guy took his shoe off and we used that for the ball. Sometimes there are more fights than football playing, with some black eyes when it's over."

Along with regular exercise periods and long marches, we also had lots of strenuous physical contact when they put one squad against another in the bull pen. The pen was about 20 feet square with three foot high plank sides. The object of the whole thing was to see which squad could throw the other out, and it lasted until that happened. There wasn't any reward for the winning squad, other than being able to walk a little taller. We were young, and just winning was incentive enough to give it our all. Another big guy and I kinda teamed up and we made up our minds nobody would throw us out. On more than one occasion three of them would try to take me, but I would lock my arms around their legs then hold on to my belt so they couldn't get me out. Sometimes they would have the backs of my legs up against the planks and God, it would really hurt, but I didn't give up. If I could get my feet against the wall I'd push off and we'd all go down. For some reason as hard as we went after one another, there weren't any fights.

Another thing they would do to put one squad against the other was the old dirt bag game. They would throw this old bag out between two squads and see which could get it back to their side. I don't remember anybody winning, just piles of bodies on top of the bag. Some guys didn't want to get that much involved. We considered them panty-waists. The rest of us didn't want to be losers.

There was plenty of competition between the platoons in shooting too. My buddy Snyder and I were in the same platoon and two of the best shots in the company. Our lieutenant would occasionally work up a little wager with a lieutenant from another platoon and he would use our talent to ease the odds in his favor. We were going out on this problem and they had different size targets along the trail. Some were big, the size of a man, and some smaller and harder to hit. Each platoon was issued a certain amount of ammunition and one hole in a target would give the platoon points. If a target wasn't hit points would be subtracted. Usually everybody would shoot at the big targets and miss or not see all the small ones. If there was more than one hole in a target you received no extra points. The lieutenant gave Snyder and me more ammunition than the rest of the platoon and told us to make sure we put one hole in each target big and small. When the competition was over we had won easily with a hole in every target. I don't know how much the lieutenant won, but he was happy and nobody except us knew he had done a little cheating.

February 17, 1943

"I came down with the measles and am in the hospital now. It's not too bad, but I had a temperature of 103. I have the German measles and they keep us separate from those with the red measles. Boy, I will miss a lot of hard work and KP."

"To answer your question, a BAR is a Browning Automatic Rifle. It holds 20 shots and weighs 21 pounds. I don't want to carry one because they're too heavy."

February 20, 1943

"Have had a lot of cards in the hospital. The sun is shining and makes me want to get outside. I sure would like to come home."

"I can not get rid of all this poison oak!"

February 22, 1943

"Sure enjoying this rest in the hospital. We're not supposed to leave, but still I sneak off to the PX for candy and ice cream."

"It's nice weather here, which makes me homesick. I would like to go out and do a little plowing or something, but I have to be inside. I still got poison oak and does it itch."

"How is my shotgun? You better oil it!"

"I hope I get one of those furloughs everyone is talking about."

February 26, 1943

"We had lots of fun in the hospital, the most since I've been in the Army. I had plenty of time to read and write letters and short sheet other guys beds. That's a little trick where we fold the bottom sheet half up so when the guy climbs in bed he can't put his feet down."

"I've been writing six different girls."

"I'm back at the barracks now, and found some of my wool blankets missing. I also got stuck with KP cause all the rest of the guys are out in the field."

"We got 40 new men from South Carolina to fill our company. They are all trained. It looks bad for us don't it. They say we'll get air raid training tonight. When the warning sounds we must get our gun and mask and run out in the field 40 yards from the barracks."

February 27, 1943

"It's been a hard time back at the barracks. Two days of KP and other details as the other men are in the field. It would be rough to come home now and I would come back to another company and wouldn't know anyone. They say when we get six months in we can get 15 days. They'll let 15 percent of the company go at one time. Boy, I would like to come home."

March 3, 1943

"I'm back workin' hard as a soldier again. We did 13 miles before dinner, then took a lot of hills and roads in training attacks all afternoon."

"Yesterday we marched 26 miles. Also we had to cross a river about 40 feet wide and 15 feet deep. We crossed on a temporary plank and wire bridge put up by the engineers.

Then we had to cross it again on a raft. The raft was built out of three tents and tree limbs. The lieutenant's raft went over and they all got wet. We had a good laugh over that. Another guy dropped his rifle in the river. One of the fellows took his clothes off and jumped in to get it. The guy couldn't get his breath and the sergeant pulled him out and asked for someone else to get it. The same guy said he was accustomed to the water now and he went back in and got it. I guess the first shock of that water was terrible."

"By the time I got back to camp I had three blisters."

"Dad, if you're thinking of buying some more land, better get some close to home. If I come home I would help like I did before, and if I don't, you will have all the insurance money you will need. Boy, would I like to be home plowing now."

"When I come home I would like to work in town a couple years, then buy me a farm, so if you and Harvey want that 40 acres, get it. I will help all I can. You know me."
March 7, 1943

"Sure was glad to get your letters. I like to hear from home."

"Next week we train with an anti-tank grenade gun. It's supposed to kick hard, but is a new secret weapon."

"The 1st sergeant said we'd all eventually get furloughs. You might see me walking in the door one of these days."

"Just had supper and five pieces of cake."

"I got soft in the hospital. That's why I got these blisters."
March 10, 1943

"They got me teaching some other guys how to shoot a rifle now."

"I sure like it now that it's not raining so much."

"I went into town roller skating, what fun."

In the town of Corvallis we had fun at the local bar. Usually there were five or six of us and we would try to find some young rookie to buy us beer. The way we did this, we all broke an egg in the top of our beer and the guy that couldn't drink it bought the beer that night.

Snyder and I could swallow them right down, no problem. The trick was to not watch the egg. It kinda floated on top as the beer went down, and when it got to the bottom if you watched it you couldn't get it down and it came back up in the glass. You bought the beer.

I don't think the people of Corvallis were that happy about having all the soldiers in town, except at the places where we spent money. It was only a 10¢ bus ride and close to Adair, so there were plenty of soldiers there every night.

March 13, 1943

"Mighty glad to hear everything's good back home. I shot the grenade launcher today and got 90 points out of a hundred. Missed one bull by just four inches. It's hard to shoot and kicked one fellow right down."

"I had guard duty for 24 hours yesterday. I took two men out to work and guarded them with real shells too. If they get away you have to finish their term, so they don't get away. We have a full clip so if they don't stop when you tell them to, you start using the shells. Boy, when you say halt, they halt. I had one guy ask me, 'You wouldn't shoot me if I ran would you?' My reply was, 'I sure would, I'm not finishing your sentence.' Most of the guys were in for being AWOL, fighting and stuff like that. If they did anything real bad they were sent somewhere else. You still had to be careful though, cause those guys carried around shovels and could knock your head off before you got a shell racked in the chamber. We weren't allowed to keep a shell in the barrel unless we were going to shoot."

"Each company is assigned guard duty once a month. We do four hours on and four off for a 24 hour period. That is not any fun as it might take you a half hour before you even got to your post. Usually ten guys or so would go out with the 1st sergeant and he'd drop off a guy at each post. If you were at the tail end of the line you might have to walk a mile and a half before you reached your post."

"I rolled dice today, but lost three 25 cent shakes in one minute. I do have a lot of fun here."

"I like the Army all right, only some things they do don't make much sense."

"My best friend Snyder has his wife staying with a preacher in town. I got my uniform all pressed and I'm going out to visit tonight. I want to look good."

"Some boys have been sent to other posts in Mississippi and Illinois. I'd like to be closer to home. The lieutenant says some of us will be going to the desert, so we should cut down on our water to get used to it."

"I'm still helping train the new guys on the rifle range."
March 18, 1943

"That stuff you sent from home sure works good on my poison oak, I'll show the doctor and they may make me an MD."

"Our lieutenant made 1st and he bought five cases of beer. We had a hell of a time."
March 25, 1943

"Today they fired machine guns with real bullets over our heads on the combat range. Sure made a lot of noise. We also shot 22s on the aircraft range and I did OK and had a lot of fun."

"I've got a little business selling candy to the guys in the field. I buy it for four cents and sell it for ten cents. A lot want it on credit though."
March 29, 1943

"We are really training hard now. Up early every day and come in late after being in the rain all day. We're also practicing packing everything just like we're leaving, even to the point of locking the barrack doors and turning the water off."

"Have also been busy with guard duty again. Wish I could take a week off."
April 5, 1943

"Slept out all week. Boy that's hard. Wet head to toe for three days. It's advance training now, and I don't like it."
April 7, 1943

"I played ball on our day off yesterday, and I was pitcher.

We won 27 to 12."

"The Army is getting harder every day. We did 20 miles this morning."

April 12, 1943

"Just keep the letters coming. I sure enjoy them."

"Slept out every night this week and I don't like that at all."

"Had KP on Monday. We have a new 1st sergeant."

"I can only buy two bars of candy now, so can't make any more money sellin' it in the field."

"Some of the fellows got in a fight after they had been drinking. I don't drink or smoke and neither does Snyder."

April 20, 1943

"About everything is wrong with me that one could get. Got more poison oak. We dug enough foxholes to tile the whole farm."

"We are learning to swim with a full field pack."

April 25, 1943

"Last night we had pie and cake for once. I ate eight pieces of pie and four of cake."

"Got up at three a.m. and had to go out and sleep in a tent. There were three men in the tent and it rained a lot, but I didn't get wet."

"Yesterday they shot machine guns over our heads again and we had to crawl on our bellies through barbwire in the mud. Keep Harvey out of the Army. It's a hard life, and no place for a man or boy."

May 1, 1943

"We had to run 300 yards and I was first in my bunch. Did it in 49 seconds."

"We got paid on Friday, and one guy went AWOL and hasn't returned yet. Someone saw him in town, drunk."

May 4, 1943

"My feet and poison oak are better now."

"What crops do you have planted this year and where?"

"I am telling you again, if you have to buy a farm to keep

Harvey home, you better do it cause the Army is no place for a Heppe. I mean it. I can take it, and so could you Harvey, but you would just waste a couple years of your life, and you might not be the same when you come home. The Army is OK by me, but it is the way they run it that gets me, and who runs it."

We got all the hills in Oregon packed down and the roads all wore out, so I guess they thought we should have some new and bigger ones. They sent us to Fort Lewis, Washington to see if we could do them in.

Well they did seem to have bigger hills there, and it was a lot colder too, especially when we were out all night. Now I was in I Company, 383rd Regiment, 96th Division.

May 9, 1943

"They say we will move to Fort Lewis in Washington next week."

"A Company F man blew his head off. Two or three others shot themselves too. Just can't take it I guess."

"I don't know who the girl is yet, but I'm going to get married when I get out if anyone will have me."

May 13, 1943

"It was a hard trip to Washington in the back of a truck. This camp is a wreck. There are no foot lockers or a place to hang clothes. The buildings are old cement buildings and the floors are cold."

May 16, 1943

"Snyder and I went to Olympia and had to sleep in a room with 250 others. No hotels were available. We had oysters for dinner and supper too. We walked around the capital and saw the waters of Puget Sound. Looked like any other water. The land here is all hills and trees. Lots of logs everywhere. The river is full of them and a couple trains are loaded up too. The logs are big, eight or nine feet across and as long as our barn."

"Snyder sits writing beside me. We've been arguing which is better, dairy or beef farming."

May 18, 1943

"We went out for training and did four miles in 48 minutes with full field pack and rifle. Boy, it is hard, but there will be a lot of them along the road with bottoms up before I fall out. I lost four pounds and am down to 198. We sleep out two nights a week. It gets harder each day."

May 20, 1943

"Mother, I received your most welcome letter, and it was a very nice letter too. Those kind of letters make me wish I was home, and now."

"They have the biggest mountain I ever saw up here, and it has snow all over it."

"Well, I hope you don't have any bad dreams about me. I dream about home a lot. They say we are going to sleep out most of the time now. We are a tough lot. We used to train as a platoon, but now we are training in bigger groups, company, battalion and regiment type operations."

"Mother, all I ask is that you don't worry about me. I will write and be thinking of you all the time and about taking care of ourselves. That's what they are teaching us now. They tell us about once a week it is for us that they are training us so hard. They want us to be the best so we will win and come home again. They say anyone can fight, but this is to take care of ourselves."

"I had two beers tonight. I feel like I am coming down with a cold, otherwise I wouldn't have taken them."

"There doesn't seem to be any poison oak here and mine's all gone. My feet are OK too, so for once I'm 100%."

"They say we will all get furloughs next month."

"We are supposed to spend most of June in the field. We are real cave men now. A lot of our training here is hiking to different objectives and not getting lost doing it. I never saw such big trees. When you come up on a fallen one, they are too big to go over. You have to go around them."

May 22, 1943

"I got six hours sleep in three days. We hike 25 to 30 miles until 4 a.m., then attack. Only eat two times a day, and it is damn cold at night. We don't even unroll our packs to sleep. It is wet and cold."

"They say now that five of us are going to be leaving. Where we will go I don't know, back east or maybe on furlough."

"They won't tell where we are going. I wish I could get close to home. I'm all packed up and have turned my rifle in."

"Snyder's wife is here working in Tacoma. So far he is not on the list to go."

May 30, 1943

"I am supposed to leave next week and am separated from the others, and doing nothing, just waiting."

"Don't worry about me going overseas, cause I don't think I'm going."

June 2, 1943

"I'm still at Fort Lewis. I bet the war will be over in six months. I am glad to get a chance to go. Almost everyone wishes they could go with me. The sergeant said he would give up his stripes to go."

On the 4th of June I was sent from Fort Lewis to join the 184th Infantry Regiment, Company G, 7th Division at Fort Orde in California. This outfit was an Army National Guard Unit from Chico, California and slated to go overseas. They were drawing men each month to fill out their company.

There were several that went from Fort Lewis, but I didn't know any of them. Of course the guard fellows all knew each other and were buddy, buddy. We were just draftees from Michigan, Ohio, Tennessee and several other states. The guard guys treated us like we had some kinda disease. Even though I didn't know the other draftees, we kinda stuck together because we had common experiences in our training.

At Fort Orde we did some gun training and a lot of amphibious work, learning how to take beachheads. They really had a lot better Army here and believed in riding in trucks rather than walking everywhere like we had to do before. It made more sense to me, learning how to fight instead of wearing out our feet.

June 6, 1943

"I am here in Fort Orde, California. It lies between Salinas and Monterey by a little town called Seaside. I was too good a soldier back at camp, otherwise I wouldn't be here. My friends are all broken up now, and Snyder is still in Washington."

June 7, 1943

"In this company I'm all by myself. I don't know anyone. I am homesick for my friends."

"We took a special train down here and I can't tell you what we do because it's a military secret. It might mean our lives so I won't write about it. I'll tell you when the war is over. What we are doing here, though, is the hardest training in the Army."

"We left Fort Lewis at 8 p.m. Friday, and arrived here at 8 a.m. Sunday. It was a swell trip, and though I didn't see any corn, I saw mountains of rocks and lots of sawmills and rivers running through the mountains. There was still lots of snow in the mountain passes. Further south I saw orange and plum trees and lots of sand. I saw the Pacific Ocean today, and it's bigger than hell. It looks deep too."

"They have good eats, but I don't know anyone yet."

June 13, 1943

"Uncle Albert from San Francisco sent me five dollars and wants me to come visit if I can."

"We do lots of sea work here, practicing taking beaches. I went out in a boat for 12 hours and got really seasick. I'm still not over it. I didn't let anything come up, just laid on my bed all the time. There was less chance of throwing up that way. A lot of them did let her come up, even the sailors. These flat bottom boats are the worst for coming up on beaches."

"The last bunch of boys here went to Attu in the Aleutians, so you can see what we are in for as they had it pretty bad."

"I hope we get in battle soon, because the war is almost over and I would like to see a little of it. I think I will too."

"Sure have got my feet wet a lot here, every time we land."

"Say, the waves here are pretty big. You wouldn't like our

little boat. The waves went half over the big boat we were on, and I still have a hell of a headache from that. I would never go into the Navy."

"This outfit isn't made up of parade soldiers like the last one."

"I'm sending $75 home and that should make $700 I have. Use it to help pay your bills, I don't need it here."

"Does Frank want to sell his farm yet? I might be able to buy it with my own money."

"I haven't got any letters from home. Mail hasn't caught up with the move. I'm getting homesick for a letter from home."

"Hi Harvey. I haven't seen any place I like as well as Michigan. The houses in Michigan look a lot better and so does the land. Have you planted the corn yet?"
June 14, 1943

"We have more time to ourselves in this outfit than we had in the others. I don't look to be here very long."

"I haven't got any mail yet and it worries me."

"Say, the sun came out today and it was really warm. The sky sure is blue. I haven't seen much sky in the last six months so I look at it now a little."

"We have a lot more new men now. A bunch just came in from mountain training in Colorado. I can't tell much, otherwise I'll be giving away military secrets."
June 16, 1943

"I like this camp. I feel better than I have for a long time. If I can just get to see Albert in San Francisco."
June 19, 1943

"I got my mail last night. Sixteen letters in all. I sure was busy reading them. So, you are about out of the hole? Well, when you get all your bills paid up let me know, and I will go out and have a good time."

"Say Mother, you do write the best letters any soldier boy could get, and I mean it. I always look for your letters. I know they will be there, and you sure can make them read just swell."

"How are the wheat and barley coming and what about the oats? How old is Jake now? Does he get around much?"

"Lots of fruit in the Army, more than at home. Plenty of apples, oranges and peaches all the time."

"This is a tough outfit, but we don't train as hard and get to ride in trucks."

June 23, 1943

"Say, you should see the mail I get now. Four letters yesterday and three from girls. I will send you a picture of that girl in Kansas I write. She goes to nurses school. Boy, is she good lookin' and writes a lot too."

"We are taking a boat ride tonight and tomorrow, so I will be seasick again. Also am learning how to shoot the BAR. (Browning Automatic Rifle)"

June 20, 1943

"I was on KP today. It was great. I had it pretty soft and all the pork chops, banana pie and ice cream I wanted to eat."

"I got into poison oak again, but am getting shots for it."

June 25, 1943

"I shot the BAR today and missed shooting expert by nine points. It shoots like hell and hard to hold. It fires 20 shots in seven seconds."

"I didn't get seasick last time out. We even had a little fun. Some of the boys saw a shark."

"So you got only 18 acres of corn in? What will you do with all the cattle now?"

"That girl in Kansas sure likes to write. Got a big letter today."

"I sent a box home today with K rations in it. Eat some and see how you like them. I don't. We had some last time out and I didn't eat them. It even makes me sick to look at them."

"I feel swell up here with lots of rest and no worries. I can rest here, the other camp had you worrying all the time. I get to bed every night by eleven thirty."

June 27, 1943

"I shot expert with the BAR, 190 out of 210, not bad. Worked until 12:40 last night unloading boats. I didn't do too much, you know me, the gold brick."

June 29, 1943

"I have it soft here, plus the squad leader likes me."

"I must send my personal things home, so save them when you get them. Don't let them brats, my brothers and sisters, tear them apart. Put the pictures under lock and key in my bedroom and hands off. I will take care of them myself."

"Say, how is my shotgun now? Maybe Harvey should oil it up and clean it too. Put it back again, I have plans for it, Ha, Ha. See how many boxes of shells I have. I may need them next fall."

"I see lots of shows here. They only cost fifteen cents. I gamble a little, Take after Dad I guess."

"I wrote a letter to Kansas tonight, and what do you think? She milks cows and drives tractors too."

"By the end of the year I might have made $1000. If I go across I will have half my pay sent home. When I get out I will have a nice nest full of eggs, Ha, Ha. I will have to find some nice hen to set on them. If I was to get married today, I wouldn't know what girl to ask. I haven't come across the right one yet, but I might see one on my road to victory."

"They've got a lot of ducks down here, and jack rabbits, but I haven't seen any pheasants. There aren't many trees, mostly sagebrush."

"My poison oak is about gone."

"You might think I am tough, but I am the same. I get along with everyone and I don't run around or drink beer and smoke either. I don't see much sense in raising hell, and maybe get in the guardhouse."

Some of the guys in my squad found out the hard way what it was like to get in trouble. One got in an argument with the mess sergeant, and afterwards went out after dinner and drank a bunch of beer. When the sergeant told him to get out of his bunk and get going he told him to go to hell. That sergeant told him he would give him one more chance and the guy still refused, so that sergeant got the 1st sergeant who gave him the same order. When the guy refused again, they called the MPs and court-martialed him for refusing an order. They just didn't give you ten days either. Everything was six weeks in the guardhouse. Those boys got up early every morning and worked like hell. When they weren't carrying a shovel they had to wear a pack every place, so by the time they got out they were in as good or better physical shape than the rest of us. That didn't sound like fun to me.

June 30, 1943

"Boy, I wish I could get a furlough before the dark days come. We are about ready to go. I see an amphibious force has landed in the Solomon Islands. Some day we might do it too, like they did."

"I sure hated to send my pictures home because I liked to look at them a lot. We don't know where or when we're going over, but it looks bad. I am glad to be able to fight if we go. I wouldn't want my grandkids to know that I didn't see any action. I don't want too much, because war is tough."

"Our packs weigh 130 pounds now."

"I wish the Japs would fly over this camp. They sure would catch hell because they got anti-aircraft guns here with men on them 24 hours a day."

In this time frame the Japs were doing a lot of things that the public didn't know about. A lot of the time we didn't even know about it either. For one thing, from their submarines the Japs were turning balloons loose that carried incendiary explosives. They would come down in Washington and Oregon and start forest fires. I don't think the Japs knew whether they were doing any good or not because it wasn't in the news. The truth was that they were being effective. Also I heard one of their submarines surfaced and shelled a refinery in California, and people really went nuts. That didn't hit the news either. The government was concerned about sabotage too. After Dad got laid off at the factory he got a job guarding a rail bridge west of Ionia. That lasted for quite awhile, until things got more secure.

July 6, 1943

"Harvey, send me that picture of Jake taken in the yard on

the west side of the house. That was a swell picture of him."

"I might not write for a couple weeks or a month if they send me across. We leave Friday I think."

We were supposed to ship out overseas real soon, and they were giving out more passes on weekends. I wanted to see Albert in San Francisco before I left, so I put in for a weekend pass. My pass was turned down. It really made me mad, because all those National Guard guys wanted to go home and see their mommies, and because we were draftees, and didn't have family close, we couldn't go. I was mad and told the 1st sergeant I wanted to talk to the captain. This was a pretty brave thing for a private to do, but the sergeant gave me permission. I was pretty nervous when I went in to see him. In front of his desk I stopped and saluted. The captain was doing paperwork and didn't look up for a couple minutes while I held the salute. He finally asked what I wanted, and with every other word being "Sir", I asked for the pass. By gosh, he gave it to me and I was off to visit Uncle Albert.

It was 120 miles up to San Francisco and by the time I got up there we didn't have a lot of time. Albert did give me a full day's tour all over the town. I rode the cable cars, saw Fisherman's Wharf and had a lot of great food. It was a fine visit and I needed it.

July 10, 1943

"We shot our guns again this morning. Everybody has to qualify again before we are sent overseas. They all qualified one way or another. If one guy didn't have enough holes to qualify, someone else would make sure a few more holes appeared so he would pass. Not enough to make him expert, just to get by."

"You should see all the things I have now. I guess we will be going soon."

"Say, how much hay have you got in now? I am glad you have the corn taken care of. Well, keep the home front going and I will take care of the battle front."

"I don't sleep much anymore. I don't go to bed until about twelve at night. Received a letter from the girl in Kansas, and one from Hattie too. I received one from Barbara yesterday."

"I've been writing eight letters a day, as I have lots of time. Pretty soon my mail will be censored and then I can't write about much."

"I will be glad to get in a little action, but I hope not too much, Ha, Ha. War is hell if you have to be on the line very long. We might be lucky and not have to do much."

"Mother, I'm glad you like my letters because I try to do right with you. I like to write home a lot as you can see by now. I might not be able to do so after awhile. I was on guard duty tonight and took some prisoners to supper. I think the war will be over soon."

"I haven't been to church yet here, but I was going last Sunday if I hadn't visited Albert. I haven't got any Bible so send one if you will. I might get one yet, as I have everything else."

"Don't worry about me smoking or drinking. I have lots of chances here to do both, but I don't. The boys want me to go to town with them every night, but I don't want to get in trouble like they do. They have fun but that is the hard way. After the war I'm going to have fun when I get home. My will power is harder than hell, you know that. I am nobody's fool, and I am pretty good with guns too, so watch out Japs. You better feel sorry for them."

"Say, that girl is good looking from Kansas, and smart from her letters. I have been writing her a long time. You should see her letters. She had a boyfriend in the Army, but I guess he wrote he wanted to go out with other girls. She feels bad I guess. She went with him for two years before he went to the Army, and she said it took him only five months to find out he had wasted two years of his life."

"I do play cards a little. I hope you don't mind that. I don't shoot dice any more. I lost three dollars one day in about three minutes. I played cards until about 3:30 this morning. I made four dollars."

"Did you get what I told you about my money if some Japs happen to be lucky. I want you to give each of my brothers

and sisters 100 dollars, and you and Dad can have my insurance and come out and see all the Army camps I have been
in, Ha, Ha."

Overseas We Go

We got on board the ship the 11th of July, 1943. It was one of those new hot dog ships from California that they called liberty ships. The only good thing about them was that they were new. This one was named the Henry Failing. If you left the first name off that proved to be a fitting name, because we heard later it broke up in a storm at sea.

By the time dawn broke on the second day 99 percent of the boys were seasick. I was sick for three days and couldn't eat or drink anything. We slept in hammocks eight deep, and I had a top one which was good. The guy on the bottom was closer to the mess on the floor, plus he had to be careful about sticking his head out too quickly in case there was someone sick above him. The place smelled horrible.

After two days they got me to go to dinner. They said that was my only hope, and that some of the others were feeling better and I would too if I ate something. With my tin cup and plate I took my place in the long line.

As you entered each compartment of the ship you had to step up about a foot and a half to go through the hole. There were a couple of sailors at each compartment door so if the ship got hit in that area by a torpedo, the sailors would close the door and seal it off. If you were unlucky enough to be inside you'd drown.

Well, I got to the food, if you could call it that. It was old boiled potatoes with the skins on and some hard beans that were half cooked, plus coffee. The ship was rolling good, and our legs were still for land yet, so you can imagine 2000 boys walking down a hallway and each one spilling some of his coffee and food. As the ship rolled one way the coffee and slop would go in that direction, then pretty soon it would be headed back as the ship's position changed. The two sailors at the door tried to help us over the doorway into the eating area and we took our places standing about four on each side of the tables. The table had a wooden rail on it to keep things from sliding off. As I put my plate down, across from me a boy's plate slid away from him to the end of the table. Pretty soon it slid back and as it came past him he threw up in it. That was all the dinner I needed that day.

The garbage can came sliding down the wet floor so I dumped my food in it, and then dunked my mess kit in the wash tanks that were slopping all over the place. I headed to my hammock for another 24 hours.

The next day I was much improved, but instead of going to the mess hall I asked a friend to get me a box of Hershey almond candy. I stayed in bed and ate that and felt a lot better.

The ship smelled bad the whole trip. There was so much junk on the floor that it couldn't be cleaned good. The toilets weren't much better. They consisted of tanks about one and a half feet wide and a foot deep with two planks spread across the top with holes cut out for your butt. The ship continually pumped water into one end and it drained out the other. You had to be careful where you sat, cause if you were at the wrong end and the ship rolled, you could easily get a butt wash.

Life on the ship was about the same every day. It seemed that all we did was wait in line, either to eat, pee or get paid. There were so many of us that they only had time to line us up for two meals each day. Every day they called your name to see that you were still there, and that seemed kinda dumb, as it was hard to jump ship out there in the Pacific.

July 20, 1943

"Well, I guess you will be surprised to hear from me again now. I am OK, but I was terribly seasick for some time. I would give $500 to get on land."

"Say, get them beef steaks fried. I will be home for Christmas dinner."

"This letter will be censored so I have to be careful what I write. I don't want to get in trouble."

We were on our way to the Aleutian Islands and were to attack the island of Kishia on the 15th of August. First we landed at the island of Adak to get things ready. Adak had an airfield, but few facilities. We had brought barrels of aviation fuel up with us and we rolled the barrels over into the water and they floated to shore.

July 27, 1943

"I guess I can tell you I'm off the boat now."

"Caught two little fish, there are lots of them here."

"I will get some mail next Saturday. First time in a long time."

August 6, 1943

"I received the Testament today and a card from Harvey, and a letter from Hattie. That is all the mail I've gotten so far. It takes a long time to get mail here I guess. Today is the first time I've had to write since the last letter I sent you. I was on a boat again so by now I'm a sailor. I bet you think I don't write much but we work hard here and don't have time to write."

"The fish are running here now. The boys get some every now and then."

"Well, I guess Dad's birthday will be over by the time you get this letter, but anyway I wish him luck."

P.S. "Keep writing. Someday I may get the letters."

August 12, 1943

"Received a letter from Robert and Harvey, and 10 from Kansas. I am swell here but we have had lots of rain and mud. I haven't much time to write or much to write about, but I thought I would write every chance I get. Tell me about what's happening on the farm."

The 32nd had come up here ahead of us and fought the Japs on Attu Island. Kishia was supposed to be a main Jap base and we expected a big fight. On the 15th we got on small LCI boats and landed on Kishia which wasn't far away. There was fog and light rain that morning when we went ashore. The navy didn't want to get stuck on land so they walked us out in about three feet of water. Boy, was that water cold. When it hit my crotch and belly the shock just about took my breath away and I thought I would have to get back on the boat. There was no fire or anyplace on shore to get warm either.

We just spent the whole day looking all over that island for Japs, but there weren't any. That was good, because someone would sure have been killed if there had been. Nobody knew ahead of time that the Japs had left. Our navy was supposed to be watching the island, but sometime in the night and fog the Jap navy came in and hauled off all their people.

The Japs left a lot of guns and equipment. They must have left in a hurry. Anything that looked interesting enough to touch might be rigged with explosives so we had to be careful. Several boys were killed from these booby traps. One gun on wheels blocked the entrance to a cave and when some boys moved it to get in the cave out of the rain, it blew up and killed them.

Our pilots out of Adak had really shot up the Japs while they were here. Anything bigger than a five gallon gas can had a hole in it. The P-38s were only 10 minutes or so away so it was convenient to fly over from Adak and pound hell out of them. The Japs were trying to build an airfield on top of one of the hills and had a narrow gauge rail and hand carts to haul rocks. They also had some bulldozers and trucks that were all shot up. The 50 caliber shells went right through the engine blocks. I even saw a bicycle shot up, and a small gun barrel had a hole right through it. That was real unusual. The bullet must have hit the barrel at a perfect angle.

On the far end of the island at the harbor there were several burned out ship hulks. The vegetation was kinda like tundra and you could see the Jap paths through it with a foxhole about every fifty yards for cover. You could see one long strip in the tundra where a P-38 caught a Jap out in the open and walked the bullets up after him.

Even though there wasn't any fighting, life sure was miserable. The weather was hell and we were always cold and wet. I don't know why we weren't all sick, but hardly anybody was. At night we didn't have any tents to sleep in, just ponchos we could buckle up into and with the rain suits and wool sweaters we could keep warm and windproof even if we couldn't be dry.

One night I dug a slit trench and had my poncho all tucked over it to keep the rain out. In the morning the poncho sides had filled with water and slipped down the hole. I wondered how I could get out of there without getting soaked. I pushed up one side real fast, but the edge slipped back in and dumped the water on me in the hole.

As I said, we did lose some men to booby traps, and we also lost some more when our own boys shot them by accident. I guess they got spooked at night and mistook someone moving in a poncho for a Jap.

One of our P-49s had been shot down on Kishia. The biggest part left was the motor and the rest just pieces of wreckage. The Japs had put up a little pile of rocks with a sign on top that read, HERE LIES A BRAVE AMERICAN PILOT THAT DIED FOR HIS MOTHER-LAND. That was the best thing I ever saw them do for us. Later a picture of this appeared in *Life* magazine.

They thought that maybe the Japs had moved to another island so my company was picked to go to three more islands in the Aleutians, Rat, Bouidler and Amtiake. We traveled to the other islands on a small raider ship that could hold two hundred men. The wind on the Bering Sea was terrible. We had to eat on deck and one morning the wind blew the milk and cereal right out of my bowl. Sometimes the waves would go right over the deck. At night we had to sleep with one arm in the rope on the side of the hammock to keep from falling out.

We didn't see any Japs, dead or alive, just one of their airplanes that had crash landed on the shore, but no one was around it. We walked all over the hills of these islands and it always seemed uphill. You would think you could see the top of the hill in the fog, but when you got there it looked the same and just went up some more. Sometimes there was a little snow on the higher spots.

When we found out we were going to the Aleutian Islands they told us there was a girl behind every tree. Well, as you can guess there weren't any trees or girls, just the tundra type bushes that made it seem like you were walking on hay. What we did see were lots of ducks and geese, more than you could ever shoot. One island had plenty of sea lions and all of them had a lot of fox. The fox weren't even scared. Our sergeant caught one but the navy said he sure as hell wasn't bringing it on their ship. We found a corrugated steel shack with a sign on it, ALEUTIAN FUR COMPANY. Later we asked some questions about it and found out that the fox has been planted on the islands and that about every five years someone was put on the island to trap them.

After we finished tramping all over the islands looking for Japs they put us back on the ships. We didn't go anyplace for a couple weeks, guess they just didn't know what to do with us. The ships really did seem like home now, after our hard shore duty. We had a lot of time to relax and fish. They even had a little crabbing operation going here. Using the ship's winch they lowered this iron loop with a net over it to the sea bottom. Meat was tied to the center of the net and after a couple of hours they would raise her up full of crabs. Cooked in kettles of boiling water, they really were good. We also got some sea bass. They were used to being pretty deep in the sea cause when they were raised up fast their eyes would pop right out from the pressure change.

September 1, 1943

"I am swell here. I received my mail yesterday and got 27 letters, five from you and seven from Elrena. She writes three pages every time on both sides. She works in a telephone office now, but would like to go to nurses training, though her mother doesn't want her to go. She sure seems like a swell girl but I haven't seen her yet."

"I can't tell you where I am, but you might give it a good guess. I sure have a lot to tell you and I have been to a lot of places so far."

"Mother, I am sure glad that you have your house all painted downstairs now, because that was what you always wanted and one should get all he can out of life when he can I guess. Say, I have that little Testament in my shirt pocket yet, but it got wet and isn't so good now. Everything I had got wet. I received the testament overseas and that was kinda funny as I got it, but none of your letters. Say, I wish Dad and you could take a vacation. You sure need one. I need about thirty days too. Ha, Ha."

"I received that stationery today, and it couldn't of come at a better time as you can hardly get it up here. We don't have movies on any boat, and I have been on a lot of them."

"I haven't been paid since June, and I only got $10 that

month. I still have 30 dollars left. I have about as much as the rest of the company here, but they don't know it. I had good luck playing cards on the boat coming over here and haven't played since."

September 3, 1943

"Well how is the best family that a soldier boy could wish for coming? I am swell. Sorry the oats are poor this year. I hope the corn comes out better."

"I know how to peel potatoes. Me and four other boys worked over 1800 pounds today. Lots of potatoes isn't it. There's usually about 285 to 300 to 100 pounds."

"How are the pheasants this year, and ducks too? Boy, would I like to put my barrel on one of them. How is Jake this summer?"

"Well I don't know what to write, you know the censor will cut it all out anyway I guess."

It took awhile, but the draftees all seemed to fit into the unit pretty good now. The platoon sergeant and I are good friends and the platoon guide and I have been good buddies since California.

Finally they decided they didn't need us up here and we were on our way to the Hawaiian Islands. It was a pleasant trip and the weather was really nice. The trouble was that all we had to wear was this heavy cold weather gear, lined pants and winter boots. I finally got sick of it and cut holes in my boots to give my feet some relief. A captain saw me do it and said that I would have to pay for those boots. He took my name down, but he wasn't from my company and I never did have to pay for them.

Everybody got sunburned on the way to Hawaii, and the saltwater showers we had didn't help much. The officers had freshwater showers though, so a few of us proved we were as smart as those officers were. We just took off our clothes, put a towel around us and walked right in and showered with them. They never did catch on.

As the ship approached Oahu, Honolulu was on one side and the open sea on the other. Everybody wanted to see the city and crowded over on that side, which made the ship lean over a lot. The ship's captain hollered over the loudspeaker for some of the people to get on the other side. I guess it scared him a little bit too.

Landing at the port of Honolulu, about the first thing we saw was a big water tower painted like a pineapple. We also saw the ships the Japs had hit at Pearl Harbor and it sure was a mess.

Hawaii sure did look good to us, and seemed more like home. It certainly was not like the Aleutian Islands where there were no houses or people other than ourselves. The weather here was 100 percent better too. We still had our winter clothes on and I bet the people there thought we were some kind of nuts to be in those clothes when it was 80 degrees outside. I thought we were kinda nuts too.

They put us up in a camp that had been used to keep the Japs they didn't trust. We stayed in tents and the camp had a high fence around it. The toilets were really bad, small and stinking, but the worst thing was the drainage. When the winter rainy season arrived, water would run right in your tent and some would leak on your bed and there would be red mud wherever you went.

We found a hole in the camp fence so on occasion we did a little unauthorized looking around the area. Finally they did start issuing passes and we could legally leave the camp.

Passes to Honolulu were issued for weekdays as well as the weekends. There were too many servicemen just to issue weekend passes. As I recall each day a company would give out one three day pass, one two day pass and ten one day passes. Most of the time the boys would be out of money and wouldn't want the pass so it would go to the next man that did. Being a farm kid I saved my money and went every chance that I could get. It certainly was better than lying on your bunk or training in the hot sun, which were the other choices.

After we had been in Hawaii awhile they issued us some summer clothes, which was a relief. We didn't wear our stripes to town though. We usually hitchhiked our way in, and one time Colonel Sullivan, our commander, picked me up in his 38 four door Ford. With a big belly and a gun hanging down from his belt, he didn't look much like a colonel. He didn't know who I was and it was an uncomfortable ride as I had to watch what I said.

The Dole pineapple plant was in Honolulu and covered 43 acres. They had tours through it at all times of the day. The tours were free so

I went through it twice.

There were some nice service clubs in Honolulu. They had food, pool tables and organized activities. I visited Waikiki beach one weekend and saw Bob Hope. They gave us a cut rate for the show and the place we stayed at.

Honolulu wasn't the place to meet girls though. There was about 100 men to each girl, so that was worse than the gas rationing back home. The cost of everything in town was high too. A shot of whiskey was 50 cents and when you went into a place they gave you four tickets so you could only buy four drinks. If however you tipped the waitress a dollar when she brought your drink she wouldn't pick up your ticket. These places would open at 12 o'clock and close at 6 p.m. There was always a waiting line because they wouldn't let any more in than what would fill the tables, so someone would have to leave before they would let anyone else in. There would always be a couple big men at the door to handle any trouble, and there always was some trouble. Outside there would be the MPs (military police) and SPs (navy shore patrol) to take the troublemakers away. They also had a 10 p.m. curfew around town so things were kinda restricted.

When I had a pass and was short on money I went over and visited another boy from home. He was a telephone repairman and really had it good. He worked on the post and had a jeep to drive wherever he wanted to go.

On one occasion when I had a pass to go into town, this other boy who also was headed in offered to take me out to eat and pay for everything. We went into this nice place in Honolulu and had a real nice meal. When we finished he picked the bill off the table and suggested we have some ice cream at the bar before we left. As long as he was paying for it I thought that was OK by me, so we had some ice cream. When we left, he stopped by the door and paid, but only for the ice cream. Now I had never done anything like that, and didn't know he was going to do it. The difference was that he had come from New York, and me from a small place where we wouldn't do things like that. I guess it takes all kinds of people to make a good army, and we had a good one.

Some of our training took place in pineapple fields. They established a fine of 50 dollars for anyone caught stealing a pineapple. After a couple of fines we left the pineapple alone. The same was true of the bananas. They were high up, but by driving a truck alongside you could reach them, but it wasn't a good idea especially if you got caught.

October 6, 1943

"I am about the luckiest soldier in the world to have a mother like you. I am going to town tomorrow. I have lots of friends here, but not as good as when I first came in the army. You know I don't want to come home now until it is all over. I like the army pretty well. Some things are all wrong, but it is a big outfit. I have seen more country here than I ever would if I hadn't come in. It has changed my life a lot. I might never come back and be a farmer. I might even buy Albert's store in San Francisco. He told me he would like to take a vacation for the rest of his life. I don't know what I want now, I might live in Kansas. Ha, Ha."

"You see I have a lot to fight for, a swell mother, father, brothers, sisters and girl friends too. I haven't changed any. I don't drink or smoke, and I don't go downtown just to look for some old girl I would be ashamed to walk across the street with."

October 15, 1943

"I am sure glad Robert likes his school OK. He will have to go on through and be the boss in our family. Ha, Ha. I sure have seen a lot of school, only it is really a school of life itself."

"Mother, don't ever stay home on account of me, for that won't help me any. You need to see some shows to take your mind off your work and worry."

"They will be hunting pheasants pretty soon, and boy what I wouldn't give to be there. No doubt I wouldn't be able to hit one, but it would be fun just to watch Jake work. I have never yet seen a dog which I would trade for him. I still think he would know me if I would be able to come home. Maybe I can make it next year."

October 21, 1943

"I wrote Elrena that when I got out she better get the chickens and ducks off the road when they see me coming. She asked what kind of a fence she should put up."

October 23, 1943

"I guess by the time you get this letter you will be hunting pheasants. Boy what fun. I guess I won't see any this year. Ha, Ha."

November 1, 1943

"Mother, I can write that I am in the Hawaiian Islands now, and that on passes I have seen Pearl Harbor and been to Honolulu too. It is a big town, but I don't like it. Too many people there, and there are more Japs than anything else here. I got my Christmas presents all bought now. I sent them home tonight so you should get them in six weeks. I spent 30 dollars on Christmas presents. Them girls got some too. Ha, Ha. You should see what Elrena got. We have lots of rain here, and it is warm too. I have a swell tan."

November 6, 1943

"I can swim pretty good now, also float too. I don't like the saltwater so good as our lakes back home. We have good eats and I weigh about 200 pounds again."

November 8, 1943

"Up on Kishia (the Aleutians) when we first got there the sun was up until 10 o'clock at night. I can't tell you where we landed, but they sure got their share of rain. The grass was green and lots of moss on things. It was like walking on a wagonload of hay to walk on the tundra. The water was cold and good to drink and some mountains had snow on them. We could catch fish on hooks without any bait. One day we got about 14 trout in 10 minutes. Did I tell you about the flying fish I saw? I saw lots of them and they really fly too. I saw one whale, and Dad should have seen all the ducks. They would set so you could come real close. I guess they had never seen anyone before. We saw black silver foxes and lots of sea walrus too. The only souvenirs I have from Kishia is a padlock

and some Jap bullets."
November 14, 1943
  "I received a birthday card this week. This month also marks one year in the army."
November 16, 1943
  "We are doing a lot of training now."
November 19, 1943
  "I sure hope Dad gets a deer this year. Dad's letters are swell, spelling not real good, but he means well and that's important."
November 22, 1943
  "Mother, so you have money in the bank now from your chickens? Good for you, and I hope you get lots more of it, for you sure have earned it."
  "The worst Japs have been taken off this island and the rest can't cause any trouble as they only have a few places they can go."
November 27, 1943
  "Glad Dad got a deer. I bet he sure is shooting off his mouth about his hunting. I am swell after my big Thanksgiving dinner. We had dressing, pumpkin pie, ice cream, corn cake, mashed potatoes, and many other good things to eat. I also had the day off. The only light in the tent is a candle so if my writing runs together you will know why."

The Hawaiian Islands were really being built up now. It was like a giant storehouse for the war effort. Warehouses were full and more being built. Large cargo ships would bring in supplies and then other ships would take the supplies out to support the navy convoys and the island assaults. The Hawaiian defenses were also being increased. They had put barbwire and pillboxes up and down the beach any place they thought the Japs might want to land troops. We also had guns and troops up in the hills ready at all times.

We were getting a lot of amphibious training now, probably in preparation for what was to come next. They took us to the island of Maui in one trip and that was really fun. From the big boat we were put out in rubber rafts with five men in each. We didn't carry any guns, which was probably a good thing as they would have been lost. Some men didn't know how to handle a small boat, but I had done it back home so it worked all right for me. The trick was to wait about 50 yards out until a wave passed, then paddle like hell before the next one came. Once close to shore you had to jump out and drag the raft in. If you were too slow getting out the next wave would lift the back of your raft up and push it to shore until the nose hit the sand and then over you would go.

We had the beautiful beaches to ourselves as no one lived along them. It was really fun to watch the other boys trying to land, and help get hats and paddles out of the water. When it came time to go back out to the big boat, we found that a bit tricky too. When the wave came in you had to have your raft ready to move fast out past where the waves started to roll. If you didn't they would raise the front of the raft up in the air and push it back until the rear of the raft caught the sand and over we'd go.

Our amphibious training was not always fun and one exercise had a sad outcome and almost claimed my life. We were training off Maui in two ducks. It was raining and the sea was real rough with high waves. The army never seemed to care about the weather. We'd train rain or shine. The ducks were six wheeled vehicles that could go on land or water and were cheaply constructed. They could hold twelve men, but your body was about half exposed when you were sitting down. We didn't figure the tin-like sides would stop any bullets on that part of our body that wasn't exposed either. The army assigned a driver and an assistant from the motor pool to drive each duck. On the front was a 30 caliber machine gun mounted on a turret and as the driver headed the duck toward shore we would take turns shooting at rocks on the abandoned beach. The duck driver ahead successfully got his turned around before he got caught in the twenty foot waves breaking towards the rocky beach. Our driver waited too long and got us broadside of a big wave coming in. We didn't go down, but I could see another big wave coming, and I knew that would get us for sure. I was a pretty good swimmer and we all had life vests on so I was not scared of getting thrown overboard, but I was afraid I would get sucked down with the duck. I got out before the next wave hit us. The wave took me down deep and tumbled me around so that I didn't know which direction was up. Finally as I was running out of breath I saw bubbles highlighted by the sun and pushed towards the bubbles. When I surfaced I expected to get hit by another big wave, but there were just small ones now. I got within 50 yards of shore and tried to swim in, but I couldn't make it and another big wave took me under and back out again. I couldn't hold my breath and was starting to take on water. I was about to give up and the thought went through my mind that I wouldn't be seeing my mother or the farm again. When I came up again there was another boy close by. His eyes were wide open and wild-looking, and he was hollering for help. He reached out for me and maybe I could have gotten his hand, but I didn't try because I knew that if anyone was going to survive they would have to do it themselves. There was no one on shore to help either. The next time I was taken down my feet dragged on the rocks, so when I surfaced I hooked my shoe soles on a rock to hold me until the wave went back out. Then I crawled as fast as I could until I reached dry rocks. I was half drowned coughing and spitting up water. There was another boy on shore too. Looking back towards the water we could see a third trying to get out, but a wave caught him and took him out and we didn't see him again. Another man was washed up and I told the other guy, "Let's get him." The water started to take him back out again but we managed to drag him high up on the rocks and spread him out. I told the other boy to make sure the guy's tongue wasn't in his throat and I tried to pump the water out of him. His eyes were open and there was foam coming out of his mouth. He had a bad head wound where the wave had bashed him into the rocks. We couldn't revive him. I could see the guy was the motor pool driver and the same one that had reached for my hand for help a few minutes earlier.

The driver of the other duck saw us go down and radioed shore for help. There was a rail line that they used to bring garbage down to that end of the island, and in about 30 minutes a jeep came driving down the tracks with a doctor aboard. We asked the Doc if we had done something wrong trying to revive the guy, but he said that the head wound did him in. I guess only one other body washed up on shore and that's all they ever found. There were cavities under the rocky shore, and maybe the rest of the bodies washed inside them to stay. Out of the 12 men the other boy and I were the only two that survived.

December 5, 1943

"Mother, I know you said you were praying for my safe return, and I want you to keep it up because I know it helps. I can't tell you why, but I'm OK, and sure hope to keep it that way."

December 7, 1943

"They had a big church service this morning in memory of the Pearl Harbor attack. I was able to go."

"Mother, I am sorry to hear Grandpa died. I know you will miss him, but don't feel too bad because I know it is for the best. He could never get better. I always felt sorry for you because you had so much work and never got to go any place when we were little. Then Grandpa came to stay just when we got big enough so you could go. I still say there never was a better mother than I have, and Dad always did what he could for us boys too. I sure have a lot to come home to. If the time ever comes when you and Dad need help, I just hope us children will do as much for you."

December 12, 1943

"Is Harvey getting a lot of rabbits now? Remember that one winter when I got 47?"

December 14, 1943

"Mother, I was very sorry to hear that you were sick. Now Mother, I want you to take care of yourself. After all, you are my best girl, and don't worry about me or anything else because it is like you always said, I was born under a lucky star and I know that to be true too. A couple things have happened which makes me sure, so please don't worry yourself."

December 22, 1943

"It hasn't rained for some time and it is cool. The sun is warm though, and you should see the moon here. The stars are extra bright too. Well, it will soon be Christmas, and I hope you enjoy it."

December 24, 1943

"I hope you all have a swell Christmas and New Year, and I hope this Christmas brings the happiest New Year of all, when I can get home sometime during the year."

December 27, 1943

"Say, Mother, that padlock I sent home was off a Jap dugout door. I broke it off getting in. The dugout was built into a hillside and they had some shells stored in it. I didn't touch anything, because it might have been a trap. We can't write much about being up there yet."

"I went to the show in town today and also had dinner. Spent some time reading books at the USO too. I sent some more Christmas presents which you should get sometime soon."

December 27, 1943

"Dear brother, how is the old muskrat trapper coming? What are you going to do with all your money? Tell me where you got all your rats. How many rabbits have you shot this year? Say, does the rifle work yet? You better take good care of it. I think you should look at my shotgun again and clean it up."

January 1, 1944

"Say Mother, I don't like it here now. Home would be swell and I seem to get more homesick every day now."

"Dad wrote that you were feeling better. I am glad of that and I wish to thank Dad for his letter. His spelling is better. That schoolteacher must have helped him."

"I go to church most every Sunday, and a lot of other boys do too."

"I got Elrena a scarf and matching apron for Christmas. Her mother shows it to everyone that comes to their place. Her old man has lots of land I guess."

"I saw the New Year come in last night and had some fried chicken about one thirty this morning. I know a couple of cooks and I had helped them out some last night."

"Mother, I sure wish that I could get to see Katherine and Mildred again. The boys too, but I don't know why, the girls seemed to be smaller when I left and I probably wouldn't know them now. Be sure and bring my sisters up to be nice girls, and also make them boys be good."

"Dad, I sure was glad to hear from you again. Even if you don't spell some of the words right, the letters are swell. I am glad you helped Harvey set his traps. He is a good kid, and I know he helps you even more than what I did. He better save his money too."

January 7, 1944

"I was to town yesterday and stayed there the night before too. It was swell to have a warm shower and sheets to sleep between. We have cold water here, and is it ever cold."

"I sent some more presents home for the boys."

"Soon I will have six months in overseas, but it seems like three years."

"Tell Dad not to worry about that 500 dollars he borrowed. I got all the money I need here."

January 8, 1944

"I just took my pen up and thought I would write a letter to the best mother and father in the world. We have the day off but couldn't get any passes, so I thought I would read your old letters over and write you one nice one. I hope you enjoy it as much as I enjoy yours. I wouldn't trade your swell letters for a month's pay."

"The moon here at night seems to be so close and big. It is always bright too, as are the stars, and so many of them."

"I sure enjoy writing home to you all. I know that you think a lot of me, but you won't know me when I get home I bet. I have changed I know, but guess it is still me yet. I still don't smoke or drink and won't as you well know."

"We have free shows most every night, and we have had a couple stage shows put on by girls from the states. Most of the picture shows I have seen back home one or two years ago, but I still like them. Our theater is just some boxes to sit on with the sky for a roof."

"It is pretty down at Waikiki Beach, but the soldiers and

sailors have taken over. They have a couple of swell USO clubs and I have been to both."

January 10, 1944

"It sure is swell to hear from home so much. Four letters yesterday, four today, and you guessed it, from Elrena. She has been sick too."

"One of my friends from the 96th also wrote. They all have had one furlough and are now going on the second."

"Mother, I am glad that you think of me as I think your wishing must help. Someday I will write you all about it. I went to church this morning. So your hens are laying eggs already? We have some eggs here, but no milk. Eggs are eighty cents a dozen."

"Say, how is the corn king (Dad) now? Ha, Ha. How did the corn keep from last fall? Yes, I really think that Dad's handwriting is better. That last letter he wrote was swell."

January 1944

"I was in town yesterday and had some oysters and went to a show. Also sent a present to a girl back home, Francis Wilson. We had a company picture taken, I don't look very good, and you can hardly see me, but it is a good picture."

"Did Dad get his new combine? What tractor will he pull it with?"

"I bet you're having snow now, and the wind is probably blowing. We will miss the snow this winter."

"I received a prayer book from Greenville, Illinois this week. It's from the Methodist Church and for servicemen, but I don't know why they sent it to me. It is a nice one though."

In February our vacation in the Hawaiian Islands ended, and we were loaded on ships for what was to be our first real combat mission. For quite awhile we didn't know where we were headed, but finally found out it was for Kwajalein Island in the Marshall Group. They had real Japs waiting for us there.

Kwajalein

After two days at sea we learned we were to launch an attack on the island of Kwajalein, where about two thousand Japs waited. They probably knew we were coming before we did. In a briefing room they had constructed a sand model of the island and took us through it a platoon at a time to explain how we would be hitting the beach. The island wasn't very big, about 800 yards wide and 4½ miles long. It was kinda banana shaped. We had gone through simulated amphibious briefings many times at Monterey, but this was for real, and an all-army operation. The marines were attacking another island that was a part of the atoll.

We knew that there were a lot of Japs there, but we had no idea how hard they would fight or what tactics they would use. This was one of the first island attacks and no one knew exactly what to expect.

We arrived off of Kwajalein one day before the attack. Everything we needed to carry for the initial assault was distributed. From the troopships we climbed down rope ladders into the LSTs. There, we watched all day as the navy ships and aircraft shot up the island.

The LSTs were pretty good sized boats that had a ramp which opened up in the front to let out the alligators carrying the troops. About eight alligators were loaded on each of two LSTs that were to hit our side of the island. The alligators were tracked vehicles that could travel on land or water and would take us from the LST to shore.

On D day we were up early and had half-cooked beans and coffee for breakfast. Our equipment was all checked again. We could take as much ammunition as we wanted. I had taken two extra bandoliers, an additional 96 rounds, plus as the assistant BAR man I carried 100 rounds of BAR shells. That was the penalty of being a big guy, I guess.

I tried to get some sleep on the LST that night, but it wasn't very comfortable. There were no bunks. You slept on any flat surface you could find. Overnight it had been reasonably quiet, but now the navy was again pounding hell out of the island in preparation for our arrival. It was hard to believe that anything would be alive when we got there. All the palm trees were about stripped and there was a lot of smoke over the island.

Not too far from shore our LST opened up and the alligators were moved out the front loaded with troops. The alligators were spread out line abreast as they moved toward the beach. They would take us all the way to the beach. In a past landing the marines had been let out in the water and they had the hell shot out of them before they could get to shore. We were heavily loaded and would have been in the same pickle if they hadn't taken us ashore.

As we headed to shore Jap artillery scored a direct hit on the alligator to the left, and it was torn open like a tin can. I doubt anyone could have survived. We were in the second wave, three minutes behind the first. The first wave was special troops that were supposed to move in 50 yards and clear the beach of barbwire or whatever, so we could move through them.

When our alligator touched the beach we jumped over the side and hit the ground behind a sand bank. We all wore life belts with gas chambers that could be released into the belt if necessary. As I hit the ground mine unexpectedly went off and the life belt was filled with gas squeezing me. I thought for a moment some Jap had me around the middle.

There already were two dead GIs on the ground close to me, so I knew this was war. I had the feeling of being all alone, as everyone had really gotten down to escape the machine gunfire which was all over the place. In training they always yelled at us to keep our heads down. Now no one wanted to raise his head to go any place. Finally we got our squad together and started moving. The first wave of men had moved in less than fifty yards from what I could tell, but they were holding and waiting for us to move through. One machine gunner had already accumulated a foot high pile of empty shells.

There was gunfire and smoke from burning buildings and it was scary. An ammunition dump had been hit by the navy and every so often there would be a secondary explosion from the dump. After each explosion live shells would be blown out and 10 seconds or so after hitting the ground they would explode. We didn't see any Japs but had the impression there were still a lot left after the navy's bombardment.

During the morning we moved in about 400 yards and set up a line completely across the end of the island. The island at that point was probably only 600 yards across. We didn't see any Japs, but they were sending plenty of bullets in our direction, and we were firing back where we thought they were. This line was established so that they could unload the boats and bring in the supplies and larger guns we needed for the push down the island.

We dug in for the night. It was worse than what we had experienced during the day. You couldn't see, but you could hear things. Some sounds were real, some you just thought you could hear. As the island was banana shaped, our position was on the inside of the banana. Where the island curved around, the Japs had set up machine guns. All night they were intermittently pumping bullets across the water over our heads. In between bursts they would shout over a loud-speaker, "Hello GIs! All you Americans will die." The voices didn't sound that far away. They were trying to get us to fire at them, and like dummies we did, each time giving away the position of our line and giving them a good target.

The first night seemed so long. One object would catch your attention and you'd look at it long enough that you'd believe it was moving. They came up close to us and would say "Hey Joe, over here Joe." We knew it was the Japs, but it still made the hair on the back of your neck change color. Where they picked up this Joe bit I'm not sure, maybe from the GI Joe army paper. I never got to talk to any of them about it.

The next morning we started moving out again and learned the hard way how the Japs planned to fight. When we first started getting shot at from behind, we thought it was our boys on the beach. Angry, we were ready to return fire at them when from about 20 feet away a Jap raised out of the ground to shoot at my sergeant and me. I could feel the gun smoke hit my face, but he missed us both. My sergeant shot back once, but I didn't have time to swing my gun around and get the safety off before the Jap disappeared into the ground. The Jap had covered his hole with palm leaves, but we found it and I dropped in a hand grenade.

I asked the sergeant how he had gotten a shot off so fast when the Jap appeared. He said his gun safety was off already. My safety stayed off after that.

About five minutes after we saw that first Jap I found another hole and fired a couple of times into the leaves that covered it. The Jap shot right back out of the hole making the palm leaves rise up about two feet. Startled, I jumped up about the same distance. We didn't have enough grenades to use in all the holes, so from then on when we came upon one of their holes we would bend over and fire in two or three rounds. The Japs would sit in the holes with their knees up and a rifle between them. If you bent over and moved the palm leaves first you would be dead, so you shot in first. Some holes were empty, some were not, but you had to shoot in all of them to make sure. If you missed seeing a hole and walked by it, there was a good chance you were going to get shot in the back. They would pop up and shoot once, and then quickly go back into their hole. Therefore a lot of times you didn't know from where the bullets were coming.

We had this guy from New Jersey that was really driving us nuts. He would follow along behind us a ways and periodically start firing into the same holes we had already done. The noise from behind would startle us, and when we asked him what the hell he was doing, he said, "Just makin' sure." We told him if he didn't quit doing it, we were going to knock his head off.

The Japs also had a lot of tunnels. Sometimes we would be right on top of their tunnels and could hear them underneath. When we found the tunnel entrance we would have one GI fire a BAR into it. Just pulling the trigger once would send in twenty rounds in about two seconds. If that didn't work, we'd throw a grenade or two in until we didn't hear any more noise. Some Japs that the grenades didn't get would run out the other end of the tunnel and we'd shoot them. It didn't really matter how we got them, as long as they were dead. There might be as many as eight or ten in one hole.

At another tunnel I stood at one end while a GI put a flame thrower into the other end. A Jap finally crawled out with his clothes mostly burned off. He looked up at us and started to crawl back into the tunnel. My sergeant put him out of his misery with his tommy gun. It seemed to me that dying in those tunnels was a cheap way to go. Why didn't 'they come out and fight? We never did crawl in the tunnels, because we were afraid of booby traps.

It was obvious they fought different than we did. They were backing down the island and leaving some of their men in holes to shoot us in the back. We weren't taught to fight that way. It seemed that the more we pushed, the thicker the Japs were. Of course it was a small narrow island and the more territory we covered the less the Japs had. There was no place for them to go.

There were a lot of buildings too. They had pushed dirt right up next to the walls as high as the roof. I walked up on one roof and a Jap inside started firing right up through the roof where I was. Boy, I got off real fast. There was a hole in one end of the roof with the tin peeled back. I put a satchel charge of TNT in through the hole, and if it didn't get him it gave him a good headache. I didn't look in the hole to see if I got him, because if I hadn't, he would have shot me.

At one place they had pushed up a bank of dirt almost twelve feet high, and there were a bunch of Japs behind it. I covered two GIs from about 20 feet back, as they lobbed grenades over the bank. Well, those damn Japs just picked up the grenades and threw them right back. Wow, did we ever run out of there. No one got hurt, and the next time we threw them over, we didn't do it so quickly. With a five second fuse we'd just hold them for two seconds after the pin was removed, then they didn't have time to throw them back at us.

We were moving ahead through what was left of the trees and a shot rang out and the man in front of me dove to the ground. Crawling up beside him I asked what happened that made him go for the ground so fast. He showed me a limb that had been blown off, about two feet from his head.

Two other GIs and I were walking around some buildings and eight Japs walked out about fifty yards in front of us. One of our guys laid down on the ground and opened up on them with his BAR. They in turn threw grenades back at us. I shot one of them, then I ducked behind a pile of tile with another boy. A grenade hit not too far from the BAR man, but didn't get him. From behind a pile of tile I shot one that was crawling along the ground. Another one looked like he had been hit. He laid there with a long knife and just kept stabbing it in and out of the ground, so I shot him too. About that time a Jap machine gun opened up on us from a pillbox, and the pile of tile we were hiding behind quickly started to crumble into a little pile. I dove into a shell hole on my left as did the other boy. The hole wasn't every deep though, and every so often the machine gun bullets would sail over our backs and rip holes in some tin sheets on the other side. I took only shallow breaths so my back wouldn't be up very high. The bullets were very close. There seemed to be a little pattern to his shooting. He'd let go a few rounds, stop, then let go a few more. I spotted a lot deeper hole about ten feet on the other side of the tin pile, so when he stopped shooting for a few seconds I jumped up like a cat and was in the other hole. The other boy did the same thing. From the hole all three of us crawled back to the rest of the platoon, who were waiting for a tank to come up and knock out the pillbox. We all were ok, but mad because the rest of the platoon hadn't helped us and were just waiting for the tank.

As I recall, the tanks didn't arrive on the island until the second day, and there were only four or five of them. The tankers didn't have very good visibility from inside, so they would rely on someone on the outside to pick up the telephone on the back of the tank and get their machine gunfire directed at the target. The big gun was sighted in where the machine gun hit. You could see the machine gun bullets hit the pillbox, then pretty soon the big gun would put a hole right into it. The Japs should have known the end was coming when they saw that gun pointed at them, but they wouldn't surrender.

We found a Jap tank later. It was dug in, camouflaged and in perfect position. The tank looked brand new and hadn't even been used. It was as if they had planned to use it later, but waited too long.

There were a lot of fortifications to knock out. We didn't always have a tank available, so then we'd use TNT. That wasn't so easy and could be dangerous. They were going to blow up this building and threw in a satchel charge; but it didn't go off. Either the fuse was bad or the Japs pulled the fuse out. Instead of throwing in a grenade to set the first charge off they threw in another charge and they blew the top off and way up in the air. It's a wonder we didn't get killed by the falling concrete.

The pillboxes were made out of cement about eight inches thick and they had steel rods in them every foot or so. Most of them had only one port in front from which the Japs could shoot. If you could get behind them with no other Japs nearby you could get them. The trouble was that they would build one pillbox behind another for protection.

Late on the second day two tanks moved out in front of our lines to blast some Jap positions. Unfortunately, they got stuck in the mud, and they couldn't get out. It was getting dark and we couldn't get up to where they were in the mud, so they just shot up all their shells and abandoned the tanks. The tank boys ran back to our lines and we got a kick out of that, because we found out those boys could run just as fast as a GI. That night the Japs went up and knocked out both tanks. They blew up one tank so bad I could see the whole top of the tank including the gun fly 200 feet in the air. It looked like a toy gun flying through the air.

The second night wasn't too bad except we had to watch for Japs from all directions. Some who had been missed in their holes or tunnels during the day were now trying to make it through our lines to join their troops. It was a rule that when it was dark you didn't get out of your foxhole even if you had to go to the bathroom. If you did you were likely to get shot.

Besides having to watch for Japs from all directions, I also had to watch out for that nut from New Jersey who was in the foxhole with me. He was always imagining snipers in the trees and would fire off unexpected rounds that really put me on edge. Earlier in the day he thought he saw a sniper in a tree and fired over the heads of two medics that were carrying a wounded man. Our medics were armed, so they dropped the litter and were ready to return fire. I crawled around to the other side of a log which exposed me to the Japs. That seemed safer. As I had to spend the night in a hole with this guy, I decided to take his ammunition away and save my nerves. I did that and didn't even talk to him. He laid on his back in the hole looking at the stars. If he was ever going to see a Jap, the Jap would have to be flyin' over in an airplane.

On the third day we tried to attack a big concrete blockhouse. They had cleared out 150 yards around the blockhouse so it was impossible to approach it without being seen. There were plenty of Japs inside to see us. We were lying on the ground in the tree line on the edge of the cleared-out area looking over the blockhouse, when a machine gun opened up on us. I was on the right side of a big coconut tree and another GI was on the other side. Those bullets hit so close I could put my hand out and touch where one had hit in front of me. I said to the other guy, "Boy, that was close." He didn't move or say anything. I looked around the tree and he had been shot in the head. In a couple of minutes he had taken his last breaths.

We couldn't get close enough to the blockhouse to do any good, and the mortars and grenades just seemed to dig it up more and provide more cover for the Japs in the basement. We finally just left some men to watch it and moved on.

As we pushed the Japs further down the island there still seemed to be a lot more of them. They were pouring lots of gunfire towards us, but you just couldn't see any of them to fire back. When you heard a machine gun start cutting loose you just instinctively jumped in a hole. If you stopped and looked for him so you could return fire, you would get shot. Once we were safe in a hole we'd return fire in his general direction to scare him a little.

There was one Jap sniper tied to his position in a tree. Everyone who spotted him the first time put another bullet in him. Because he was tied his body wouldn't fall down. Finally an engineer came along and cut the whole tree down.

We were traveling lighter now. We had left behind our packs, gas masks, tin plates and other things so we could move faster. We still carried our shovel, water cup, canteen, can opener, knife, spoon, rifle, rifle belt, hand grenades and lots of ammunition. That was still a good load, but you could move better with it.

In the middle of the island there was a Jap airfield that was pretty well beat up. There was no cover to cross that dumb thing, so moving out two at a time, we really had to make tracks. Amazingly, nobody got hit. I guess the Japs were just not very good shots.

I sat down to rest beside a tree that had been shot off about five feet from the top. My butt had no more than hit the ground when I heard a machine gun open up and I saw wood chips falling on me from the tree. Boy, did I ever get out of there fast. It was too close.

We moved ahead and there was a shell hole about fifty yards away. They told us to head for that hole, so we took off on a dead run for it. The bullets were hitting on both sides of us and in front too. We had our hands in front, kinda shielding our faces as we ran. Why we did this I don't know. I guess we didn't have to see all the bullets that way. Well, the last ten feet we didn't run, we just jumped straight into that hole. We were all ok. How we did it without getting shot I don't know. Once in the hole, every time we raised our heads to see some Japs, the bullets would start flying again. We couldn't do much good. The sergeant thought it was too hot and not enough cover to move the rest of the men up, so he called us to come back. We returned the same way, only we didn't put our hands in front of our faces. We couldn't see the bullets hitting behind us anyway.

While we were slowly progressing down the island, the navy aircraft bombed some docks on the other end. When their bombs hit you could feel the whole island shake under your feet. They weren't supposed to bomb within 500 yards of us. This was a good thing, because they weren't that accurate with their bombs. The navy did do good work with their big guns. They had destroyed some large guns the Japs had, blowing them off their concrete stands. You could see a lot of the navy's sixteen inch shells laying around that hadn't exploded. We stayed clear of those. The navy's firepower sure saved a lot of our lives.

We pushed up to 600 yards from the end of the island that day. Just before dark the BAR man right behind me was killed. I hit the dirt behind a shot-off tree and another guy went over to help the BAR man. He was shot in the stomach, and killed too. That was three men that had been killed right next to me that day; I learned one thing for sure, if a Jap can see to shoot one man, don't run to him as they will shoot you too. You might be only ten feet away from the man they shot, but there might be something between the Jap and you so he couldn't see you. No sense exposing yourself. Also, a tree was good for cover, but sometimes it was easier for the Jap to see you next to something rather than being in the tall grass. We learned that the best way to help the wounded was to provide cover so the medics could get in there and give some aid.

My sergeant told me to get the dead BAR boy's gun. I ran by the two dead boys and got the gun. He sent me back to get his ammunition too. On the next pass I got ahold of his belt and pulled him behind a tree. It's hard to get a rifle belt off a dead man, so the tree provided some cover while I undid it. I was the BAR man now.

We thought we might take the whole island that second day, but it didn't work out that way. We dug in for the night and the Japs still owned 600 yards.

That night they put me and the BAR between two light machine guns, so I could help protect them. The Japs always tried real hard to knock out the machine guns. I was in a three-man foxhole, but there were only two of us. The BAR man was the missing man, and the guy with me was the one from New Jersey who wasn't really a soldier. I don't know how I got stuck with him, but others had complained about him too. Later they finally sent him to the back of the lines and he didn't even get his Infantry Combat Badge. I thought any dumb GI could get that.

I took inventory of my ammunition and with what I had taken off the dead boy I had 400 rounds and nine hand grenades. When dawn broke the next morning, I had thirty five rounds left and one grenade. What a hell of a night that was. I saved the one grenade all night just in case they broke through our lines. I figured if I had to, I'd put it in front of my hole and save myself from a bayonet. I'd heard the Japs like to bayonet ya'.

The Japs were out in front of us, but real hard to see. Our ships would send up flares every so often and they provided light for a minute or two. When one went up I could see a Jap lying crossways in front of me. I couldn't see my gun sights because of the shadows, so I just looked down the barrel and let the bullets run over him. It worked. Next I saw one raise up and I moved across him three times before his head stayed down. One Jap was back of a shot-off tree and throwing grenades at us. Fortunately he had a good arm and was throwing them over my head. The Jap grenades were different from ours. For one thing they were lighter and could be thrown farther. They also would sparkle after the fuse was going so they were easy to see. They set off the fuse by hitting the grenade against their helmet after they pulled the pin.

I was hoping this guy's arm didn't get tired cause otherwise one might end up in my hole. Well, I threw one grenade at him but I couldn't see where it hit. I tried a second time and that was short. On the next try I had to raise up out of my hole and throw as hard as I could, but before I did I told the machine gun on my left to cover me. He did a nice job and my grenade got in by the Jap and when he moved away our machine gun got him.

Another Jap machine gun set up just off to our right front opened up on us. Both our machine gunners put it to him, and in about two minutes he was done. About an hour later the same machine gun opened up on us again and we silenced it the same way. Every fifth shell out of our machine guns was a tracer, and you could see that the boys had hit that gun good. Nevertheless, the same area opened up on us over and over throughout the night. In the morning we found the gun right on top of the ground in good shape with eight dead Japs around it.

Sometime around one in the morning, something hit me in my right butt. Boy, my eyes blinked open and at first I didn't dare reach down to touch the area. I did finally, and I came up with blood. I didn't say anything because I didn't want anybody to get killed trying to get me out, and it didn't hurt too bad.

Through the night we'd fire mortar shells in back of their lines. The mortars would set fires and we could see them then, moving around in front of the fire. When the mortar fires burned down there still was a red glow on the skyline which also helped us spot them.

About an hour or so after I got hit my butt was startin' to hurt a little more, but I forgot about that when the Japs started blowing a bugle. That was the most awful sound at night that you could imagine. It got completely quiet for a few minutes. You could have heard a pin drop. We had heard yelling a little before that, like they were getting high on saki or something to get their courage up. After the bugle they started to come towards us. I saw four or five run across in front of me, but didn't even get a shot off, it surprised me so. After that though, I was ready and it was all war until morning. If they had all come at us at the same time, we probably wouldn't have made it. Instead they ran at us in small groups.

As morning light broke the Japs were dug in about forty yards out in front of us. One Jap was kind of trapped behind a small mound of dirt. He'd stick his head out one side and we'd shoot and then he'd try the other side with the same results. The mound was so small that when his head showed up on one end, his rear would almost appear on the other. Finally we didn't see him and there was a small explosion. We thought maybe he had killed himself.

We were almost out of ammunition, so we weren't doing any shooting back at them. The Japs would shoot at us by raising their rifles in the air and then let the barrels come down and fire like you would a pistol. When the barrels came down you could hear all our boys' helmets clunk as they put their heads down. A lot of us didn't wear the helmet chin strap because we had heard that a close explosion could take your head off with the helmet. Anyway, that went on for some time and it seems kinda funny now thinkin' about all those helmets clunking at the same time. It wasn't funny then. Well, not too much happened for awhile and then they put up a white flag. My lieutenant was taught how to talk to the Japs, which he did for over an hour. He'd holler, and they kept waving their flag. I thought, "Gee, this is going to go on forever." They were supposed to come out with their hands up and clothes off. I always told him afterwards that he must have given the wrong order to them, cause they came out with their rifles at port arms and ran toward us fast. It was just one big ending for them. We were ready for it, and even if we didn't have much ammunition left, we did have enough for that.

It seemed about over except for the tough ones. Our 1st sergeant was trying to determine our casualties by yelling back and forth with the squad leaders. He finally raised up out of his foxhole to hear better and was shot dead. His notebook and pencil were still in his hands as he laid there. That night we had killed so many Japs that out in front of us you could walk on only Japs for twenty to thirty yards.

They brought some food up to us, and that was the first I'd had since we hit shore. I didn't have a chance to get at it though because a different kind of hell broke loose. There were three GIs walking through those dead Japs and they saw one move so they put a bayonet to him. There were some more that weren't dead and the GIs were sticking their bayonets into both the dead and live ones, and were yelling all over the place. Then another guy with a BAR would fire a round into the bodies. With the noise of the guns, the GIs yelling and the Japs moaning and squealing, it was awful. At a distance we don't look much different than a Jap, so I could see that this was no place for me. I got behind some concrete to be safe. Those guys were half mad, I think. After some time, other GIs finally got them calmed down.

We got some more ammunition with the food that came up. We moved toward a pillbox that was firing at us. We called for a tank, and when the Japs saw it coming they gave up. They came out with their hands up and wearing only their shorts. I'm surprised some angry GI didn't shoot one of them, but nobody did.

Finally I got down in a big bomb hole and tried to eat a can of beans. A Jap started shooting at me and one bullet hit the inside of my hole. There were very few trees big enough to hide a man, but I could see the leaves on one move with the next shot. I had the BAR and let the top of the tree have twenty rounds. That shut him off, though I didn't see anybody fall. Before I got back at those beans another Jap started shooting at me from a different direction. I did the same to him. Their guns don't make much smoke, and they only would shoot once then wait for awhile so it was hard to see them. I thought maybe they were short of ammunition, but we found out later they had plenty. That was just their style of fighting, I guess. Hell, we'd shoot any amount of ammunition to save one life. It was around noon and my butt was starting to hurt from the wound and it was getting hard for me to walk. The fighting was all over anyway, so they sent me back to the aid station.

Out of 5000 Japs only twenty some gave up and were taken prisoner. The rest were killed. They had a bulldozer dig out holes. They attached ropes to the dead Japs and pulled them into piles next to the holes. With the warm temperatures they were already starting to stink. They put up some kind of marker at each hole stating how many Japs were buried there. The guys were grumbling because not only did they have to kill them, now they had to bury them too. While we were fighting we didn't see many dead or wounded Japs. They tried their best to hide them so we wouldn't know how many we had killed.

I don't know why more didn't give up, whether they were scared of us or scared if they tried, their own men would shoot them in the back. I guess they knew they would never make it back home. In fact I heard that they had a funeral-like ceremony at home before they were sent out, and that it was an honor to die for the empire.

They couldn't get the shrapnel out at the aid station so I was put on a hospital ship and sent back to Oahu in the Hawaiians. Being on the hospital ship made me nervous, because at night they had it lit very bright. We were all alone on the sea with no escort. I didn't really trust that the Japs wouldn't send a torpedo at us.

While we were on the ship there was a guy beside me with a cast on his leg. He just about went crazy when he rolled over and white maggots fell out from underneath his cast. I heard afterwards that they only ate dead tissue and were good for a wound, but they sure made a basket case out of the guy. I wouldn't have wanted any on me either.

It's funny, when we were in training one of the guys, a redhead, was always saying he would get killed. He was one of the first hit, shrapnel in the legs. It shouldn't even have been a life-threatening wound, but I guess the shock killed him. I even thought it might have been one of our guns that got him. After that, I figured that if I ever thought I was gonna get hit, I certainly wouldn't say it out loud, it would stay deep inside of me.

One of our guys did get shot by his own men when he got out of his foxhole at night. You were never supposed to do that, even if you had to go to the bathroom. He got shot in the head, in fact it took off part of the top of his head. They figured he was dead and didn't carry him back to the aid station. The next morning he was still alive. I swear you could see his brains exposed in that wound. They took him back and eventually put a plate in his head. He lived, but he wasn't right after that.

I saw a lot of boys die that were shot in the stomach. That wound had to be taken care of right away to save them. If they threw up, you knew they wouldn't make it. A stomach wound didn't always look too bad, and for a day they would talk and their eyes were clear. The next day they would be dead. They had very good doctors in the army, but there were too many wounded men to take care of at one time. They sure did save a lot of lives in a very short period of time.

MRS. ELIZABETH HEPPE
=ROUTE NUMBER ONE ORLEANS MICH.

REGRET TO INFORM YOU YOUR SON PRIVATE FIRST CLASS VERNON W. HEPPE WAS ON FOURTH FEBRUARY SERIOUSLY WOUNDED IN ACTION IN KWAJALEIN ISLAND MARSHALL GROUP PERIOD MAIL ADDRESS FOLLOWS YOU WILL BE ADVISED AS REPORTS OF CONDITION ARE RECEIVED.

=ULIO THE ADJUTANT GENERAL

KWAJALEIN

February 13, 1944

"Well it has been a long time since you heard from me, but now the letters will come again."

"I have been in action, as you know, I guess. I was down in the Marshall Islands which you probably have read about. I can't say much about it yet. I got hit but not very bad, as I am around now. They hit me right where I sit down. Ha, Ha. I don't think it was a bullet, but I don't know yet as they haven't taken it out. I am in a hospital on the Hawaiian Islands."

"I was on the front a lot, and I know I shot five Japs in the daylight and I don't know how many at night. I think around twenty or more because there were lots of them and I had lots of shells."

"I have a lot of Jap money which I will send home soon, along with some other things."

"I haven't received any mail yet, but I sure wish I would."

"Don't worry about me because I am OK and can walk

around, but can't sit down very good."
February 15, 1944

"They haven't got the shrapnel out as yet, but they know where it is, just below my hipbone. It doesn't hurt very much."

"I had one Jap shoot at me and another boy from only five yards away. He missed. They can't hit anything, which I am very glad of. We got pretty close to them before you would see them."

"It was at night when I got hit, and boy I don't like it at night at all. That is hell."

"We have some very nice army nurses here which I have a lot of fun with."
February 18, 1944

"I received eighteen letters the other night. You should see the Valentine I got from Elrena. Did you get the one I sent you?"

"Today I got my Purple Heart from the general of our 7th Division. It has a picture of George Washington on it. I don't know what it is made of. I will send it home."

"They haven't taken the shrapnel out yet. I think Monday they will. Today is the first day I have been down to the mess hall. I also got my hair cut too."

"I hope they pay me soon as money is low. I got in a card game on the boat and did OK or wouldn't have hardly any now. I am lucky in more ways than one. Someday I will tell you all about it."
February 21, 1944

"I am back in bed again, when they can keep me there. I had the shrapnel cut out yesterday, and it hurt a little. I have the shrapnel yet and will send it home with my Purple Heart."

"So you liked that platoon picture of us? Well there are three you can cross off of it now."

"Those Japs are like shooting rabbits, but they can't run as fast. Say Dad, I can't cut any notches on my gun as I lost it along with the rest of my stuff when I left the island."

"Say, how do all of those boys back home get medical discharges? I should have one. Ha, Ha."

"We have some swell nurses here and good ward boys. The captain was over to see me yesterday. The colonel came over a couple days ago."

February 26, 1944

"I have been here in the hospital for two weeks. Say, am I ever glad that I am not married. Ha, Ha. I have no home worries."

"The Jap bills I am sending you are only worth about 5 cents in our money, but sailors were offering $10 for them. I got four of them, but wish I had 100."

February 29, 1944

"I was on Kwajalein Island, the biggest in the Marshall Group. The sergeant was over to see me yesterday and said we could write about it."

"The first night we were on the front line two more boys and me had ten dead Japs in front of our foxhole, and that was a quiet night."

"The next night we got hell. That morning I got hit about one or two. I didn't leave the front lines until about 9. I think I got between 10 or 20 that night. You couldn't even count them the next morning. It looked like we had lined them up and shot them down. I couldn't walk very good, my leg hurt some, but I could still take care of myself."

"For 4 nights I didn't get any sleep, and I was pretty worn out. I couldn't sleep then for almost a week. I would wake up and think the Japs were coming and that I had been to sleep at my post. It is hell at night. I never want anymore, but I guess we will have some more some day."

March 7, 1944

"Now you don't have to worry any about me as I am all right. I will be out of the hospital by the 12th. Hard to believe it's March already. The wound is healing fine. I can walk and soon will be able to run as fast as I did before. I have even put on some weight. Yes, I carried the Testament with me and I still have it here. I also have the prayer book they sent me before I left."

"Say, if I don't write you something it is because I can't. I can't write very much yet or won't until I get back in the USA. We can't tell who got killed or how many, but our company did lose some. You would only worry if you knew more about it so it is best the way it is."

KWAJALEIN DESTRUCTION (blockhouse pictured above)

Our platoon before
Kwajalein. I'm in top
row 4th from left.

Flag over Kwajalein

R&R In Hawaii

I spent three weeks in the hospital, and then returned to my old unit which was back in Hawaii also. We weren't in tents this time. They put us up in six-man wooden huts which were located in a big post with lots of things to do. This post almost seemed like a city. They had buses to take you all around and everything.

Some new men were added to fill up our company, and they had to have training so we had to be out there with them. We didn't enjoy that too much, but didn't have much of a choice.

They brought back some of the unused explosives from Kwajalein and were using that to train with. They didn't want to use the old stuff in any new battle, but figured it was OK for training.

We were all in a big circle around this instructor who was demonstrating TNT use. When he pulled the pin it went right off in his hand. He went up in the air a ways and landed dead in front of us. The charge was supposed to have a 4 second fuse, but this charge either didn't have a fuse or it had deteriorated. There was no shrapnel in it so no one else got hurt. That really made me mad because that boy's life was lost and it didn't help to end the war at all. There is a lot of waste of supplies, but to waste a life is bad. He wasn't from my company, but I felt sorry for him. I wonder what they told his folks.

March 11, 1944

"I miss your very swell letters. My mail is being held up somewhere. I wish I knew where."

"I am back with my old company, and the boys again. We have six-man huts with eight men in them. Ha, Ha. They are still better than tents. We also have lights here, but they are not very bright as they have too many on one line I guess."

March 12, 1944

"I received Harvey's letter tonight, and it was swell to hear from you all again. Yes, I have the shrapnel that hit me. I will send it home with my Purple Heart. It wasn't very big. I will put a couple of Jap bills in my next letter. I want them saved until I get home."

"I went over to see Robert O'Neil today. He was working, but I rode around in the jeep with him anyway, and also ate dinner with him. He said he looked in every hospital on the island and couldn't find me. He was at the one I was in, but they couldn't find my name on the record."

March 15, 1944

"Say Mother, why do they print my letters in the newspaper? I don't care much for that. After all I didn't do any more than anyone else, and I came out a lot better than some of the boys."

"I don't get seasick anymore. I have been on the water more than a lot of sailors, I think."

"I can't write you on how many boys were wounded or killed. You will have to wait until after I get home. Lots of things I know which I can't write about. I also found out today that I can't write a thing about Mrs. Otha Howell's son. I will go down to his company if she writes back."

"Elrena will have a birthday May 10th. She will be 20 years old, so I will look her up a present. I haven't been to town since January 19th, but hope to soon."

March 17, 1944

"Mother, I received four letters today, yours, and two from Elrena."

"Say Mother, don't put me in print too much. I don't care for that."

"Yes, we got all the Japs down there. There were lots of them too. You should have read about it back home in the paper and *Life* magazine. I saw that gun where the dead Jap laid in that picture on *Life* magazine. The general of the 7th Division pinned the Purple Heart on me in the hospital, and his picture was in *Life* magazine too."

"Now Mother, don't worry about me so much, because I am not worth it. I am just as good as before. It doesn't hurt unless I hit it or something."

March 22, 1944

"Say Mother, I received your last letter of the 12th, and it was swell to hear from you so soon. Now I don't know what was said about me over the radio, as I didn't have a thing to do with it. You will have to tell me what they said."

"Now I don't want you to worry. I was born under a lucky star. Last December I had a close one and almost drowned when a boat turned over in the ocean. I still don't know hardly how I made it out. I was under for a long time, but I didn't breathe and had only a little water in me when I got out. Some that could swim good never made it. I thought of you and Elrena and that I would never see you again."

"Dad, what I would like to do when I get out is take over Uncle Albert's business in San Francisco. He said that when the war was over he could teach me the business. First we have to wait until the war is over. I hope that isn't too long, but I don't look to be home before 1946 or maybe later."

"Now you do what you want to about buying the land. Ask Harvey now that he's taken my place. He is a swell kid, so let him help you and take my money if you want to. I don't have any use for it."

April 3, 1944

"I have been pretty busy going to shows and laying around. I have a three-day pass coming up. I have only taken one day off since I have been back."

"Well, it is April now. Have you started any field work back home yet? All they have over here is sugar cane and pineapples. They grow year-round."

"It sure is getting hard to write letters, as there isn't anything to write about. Most of the things we're not supposed to write about."

April 5, 1944

"I got your letter with five others last night."

"It told in the papers how many were wounded and killed. That was about right. About 30 Japs were killed to one of us, so you can see who came out the worst."

"Yes the Red Cross is OK. Coming back on the boat they gave us razors and candy. In the hospital you could get some money from them. They gave us V mail and books of all kinds and playing cards. When I was in the hospital a woman came around once a week and if you wanted anything she would get it in town for you. They are OK as far as I can see."

"I still talk in my sleep about those Japs, so the boys say. So do some of the others, for I heard them."

"I hurt my ankle playing ball so am on light duty now."

"In *Life* magazine March 13th on page 82 and 83 the top picture, I was there. I also walked by the big Jap gun on wheels that was pictured with the dead Jap. That picture of the general who had the 7th Division is the one that pinned the Purple Heart on me."

April 1944

"Harvey, I received your swell letter today. So you made a lot of money out of your traps this year. What are you going to do with it? You had better put it away."

"So Robert is going to start school next year. You better fix the Ford so it will only go 30 miles per hour. Ha, Ha."

"Boy, you better let those girls be back home and get to work."

April 9, 1944

"I thought being Easter I had better write you a letter tonight. I went to church today. Did you go? I don't go every Sunday, but should. I went over to Mrs. Howell's son's company last Saturday and found out what I could about how he got killed. They said they would write her, and I wrote her what I could last night."

"I saw in the service club that there is a boy here from home. They have a big map there and you put a pin on your home town. There already was one from Ionia there, so I put another one up."

April 13, 1944

"I received a good conduct ribbon last week. I have been almost one year in the 184th Infantry. It has sure been a long one."

"I don't think Bob Mellinger will be on the same island as I am. They don't put the marines and soldiers together because sometimes they fight between themselves."

"Yes, we have some very good ballplayers here. We play other companies a lot. I played last night, but we got beat 3 to 2. Last Sunday we won two games 3 to 1 and 3 to 2. Monday we won 5 to 4. I pitched in all of those games."

"I am going to try and go to town tomorrow as they have a good movie on, and also the battle of Kwajalein. It seems kind of funny that I would want to see it after being there, doesn't it."

"Boy I sure would like to get sent back to the states now. If we could all go home for 30 days, that would be something. There are a lot of boys like me who never even had one furlough yet. I have almost one year overseas and one and a half in the army."

April 17, 1944

"I played two games of ball today and we won both of them. We played H Company, and I pitched."

"Say, have you got my Purple Heart? You should have it by now."

"I am still nervous yet, and so are most of the boys. We have new boys who aren't. My ear is OK and everything else. I had a good checkup a couple weeks ago at the hospital."

"Say, if you want that 40 acres across the road, why not buy it, I don't care. You know more about it than I do. I haven't been home for some time as you know. It seems like 10 years."

"Boy, I have seen a lot since I left home. It would take a year to tell it all. I should write a book on the life of a soldier, Ha, Ha. The only trouble is, I'm not home yet."

"We have more passes than we do money. We have pretty good eats, chicken about two times a week. Free shows are available every night and we have lights in our barracks. It has been pretty soft since we came back. I just hope it lasts. Ha, Ha."

After a couple of months back in Hawaii we were all feeling pretty good. The memories of Kwajalein were still there, but we were rested and feeling good about our success. The commanders had all been through to visit those still in the hospital and numerous medals had been awarded. Then one day the battalion commander called us all out on the parade field and what he said really made me furious.

Standing out in front of the troops the colonel started going over the statistics of the Kwajalein battle. He said we had killed 5422 Japs and lost less than 500 of our men. I said to myself, "Now that's something to be proud of." The colonel continued on, "You killed over 5000 Japs but had to use over 250,000 rounds to do it. That's too many shells, men. It only takes one round to kill one Jap." He continued rambling on, but I didn't pay any attention to what he was saying. That was the dumbest thing I ever heard anyone say. You'd think he was paying for the shells. He didn't even pay for his own meals. I didn't care if it took 250 bullets to kill one Jap, if it saved just one of our boys. I always shot them two times so they would be dead, dead. I guess he thought if you missed with one shot you should run up and cut his throat. That's not for me. I like a nice clean job. I wish he had been there one night. I bet his pants would have been full and he probably would have been shooting up in the air from the bottom of his foxhole. He should have been there by that tree when Sullivan Wolf didn't answer me because a Jap machine gun bullet had hit him in the head. Maybe he would have looked at things differently if he had been there when the BAR man Eugene Engwell got cut down just behind me, and then the man that tried to help him got it too. I kept my thoughts on the colonel's speech to myself. Otherwise he would be making a 20-year man out of me and I would be moving some mountain with a wheelbarrow.

April 26, 1944

"Elrena wrote me a letter and said if she went to summer school she could teach this year. I told her to do it as that is a pretty good job. She doesn't like to work in the telephone office too well. She has to work seven days a week."

"I guess by this time you will have some oats in, or should have anyway. Did you get all the wood put up this winter?"
April 29, 1944

"I sure was lucky this week. I have received two letters from you and also a picture from Elrena, a big one."

"So you really think I am a swell boy? After all, I couldn't ask for any better Mother and Dad."

"My ankle is OK, and so is my ear, and Mother don't worry about what kind of business I get into. Since I left home I have had my eyes open and have learned a lot, and can live away from home. I sure would like to rent Albert's business in California. The 184th Infantry is from there, and most of the men from California, so I would have lots of friends there. Only time will tell."

"If Ralph Leland has my address it would be easy for him to visit me. Everyone knows the 7th Division and I am in that. 7th Division, 184th Infantry, Company G. That is all you have to know."
May 3, 1944

"Harvey, so you have over 100 cords of wood up now. You better sell some soon."

"I hope you don't have to go in the army."

"I guess you have a girl friend now, so what is her name? A boy with a car should have one."
May 7, 1944

"I will drop you a couple of lines to let you know that you are the best Mother in the whole world. I haven't received your letter yet this week. Every day I thought it would come. The mail hasn't been coming in very fast lately."

"Boy, it would be swell to put my two feet under your table again and eat. That is the life that we dream about now. We eat on tin mess gear and have ever since we left the states."
May 11, 1944

"By this time you should have had some fish to eat. Boy,

that was fun to spear them. I would like to do a little of it now."

"So Mildred is a pretty good cook now. I might need someone to cook for me when I get out so tell her to keep trying. They can't learn too young how to cook."

"I bet Katherine is getting to be a pretty big girl now, and Dad will have to keep those boyfriends away."

"Boy is it ever hot here now. I have a swell tan."

May 14, 1944

"I was on KP today and that was one job I didn't like. It was pretty hard today and I didn't even eat much."

"I am sending home a newspaper from here. We had a big parade last week and pictures of it were in the paper. I would like to come home with the newspaper. That would be a day to remember. When I left home I never thought that the war would last this long, and I ain't home yet by the way. Ha, Ha. But I am still hoping."

"How is old Jake coming now? I sure hope he lives until I get home. I often wonder if he would know me now."

"I had a tooth filled last week and have four more to fill yet. He said my teeth looked very good though. I hope that I can last as long as my teeth do."

May 18, 1944

"I saw Ralph Leland yesterday. He was here all day. We went down and saw Robert O'Neil too. Ralph knew him in school."

"I received a letter from Jerry today and he is OK. He said Donald Minikey was on Anzio beachhead, and that he said it was hell. Jerry saw his brother for the first time since 1941."

"I have my radio working now and the boys sure like it. I have a lot of friends now. We have too many men hanging round our hut though."

"So you did get the 40 acres. If I was Dad I would sell the trees for 1000 dollars. The war might get over and they wouldn't be worth as much."

May 20, 1944

"I will write your letter tonight as it is raining and I can't go to the show. I received your letter of April 29th, and Harvey's of April 28th. I will try to answer both of them. They sure are swell letters that you write. I just stop whatever I am doing and start reading them."

"I was glad you liked the birthday card and the purse, because there isn't anything too good for my Mother and Dad."

"Mother, I won't answer those questions you asked about December 3rd, as it only seems like a dream now, and I want to forget it. The battle of Kwajalein seems like a bad dream also. It doesn't seem like those things could happen in our world today."

"Yes, we all have two invasions in the 7th. That is what those two stars mean on that one ribbon. If we go back and win another battle we can wear three, but two is all I want."

"If Elrena writes to other soldiers that is OK, as I write to some other girls also. After all this is war. Ha, Ha. She seems like a swell girl, but only time will tell all of those answers."

"I said after I came in the army that I wanted to see a little action, but not too much. I had enough to last me 300 years after the first night. It is surely a big bad dream, but don't worry about me as what is to happen will happen."

"Harvey, how do you like the new farm we got now? It will give you a little more work this summer. You should get Frank's 20 acres now, and then you would have a corner of that farm. It would save a little fence and make more pasture. So you get more money than when I was working at home. I am glad that you do, as you are a swell boy and I sure hope you can stay home to keep on helping Dad. He sure needs you."

May 27, 1944

"Have you got the cows on pasture yet? Did Nelson put a fence around the 40 acres yet? Have you sold the woods yet? My letter will be all questions if I keep on."

"Have Harvey and Robert learned how to swim? The girls too. You will never be sorry."

"We don't ever have any lightning over here. Only once I saw it. We have lots of rainbows every day. It is really warm now."

"Harvey won't have to go to the army will he? I sure hope that he doesn't. He shouldn't have to, and you better see that he doesn't. He is really too young. After all he is only a kid."
May 30, 1944

"That billfold I sent home was on a Jap that was killed right behind me during the night. The next morning I took it off him and sent the money home to you. It also had some papers which I turned in. The sewing kit was in my pocket where I got hit, and you might be able to see my blood on it."

"Yes, some of Bern Howell's friends were near when he was killed. He was killed instantly and never knew what hit him. Did his mother ever write you again?"

"I spent my two-day pass Sunday and Monday at Honolulu and Waikiki Beach. There were a lot of people there Sunday afternoon."
June 1, 1944

"Harvey, have you sold the woods yet? What do you think of the new 40 acres? I sure was surprised to see that I only had $25 in the bank. Here I thought I was rich. Ha, Ha. No, it was OK by me to take it all out. I sure don't need it over here. I have half a mind to send 50 dollars more home. I only get $27.95 each month. That is all I need too."

"I heard the WACs were to play H Company a game of softball tomorrow night. I sure don't want to miss seeing the girls play if they do."
June 3, 1944

"I have had a lot of mail this week. I received nine letters last night and two tonight. I am still 100 percent OK. We had a very good supper tonight, with pie too. We played ball after 3 p.m. today and have tomorrow off."

"Say, Robert must be a pretty big boy now. He should be a good boy, look at the swell brothers he has. Ha, Ha. I am glad he likes to help on the farm. I put a couple years there myself, only I didn't have it so easy for I never had a tractor to work with."

"Boy, I would like to be home in the spring when the trees leaf out and the birds come back. Also all those pretty girls back home just waiting for someone to call them up, but the paper says that a lot of them are getting married."

"I can only get two stations on my radio, but I wouldn't take 50 dollars for it. It is swell."

"Say, I bet Robert really is a man now with his new suit on. He will be 14 years old in October, won't he? I forgot how old my little brothers and sisters are. I see Katherine is almost out of grade school too. She must be pretty big now."

"I heard from Snyder this week. He is the good friend I had in the 96th Division. They are in California now and it might not be long before I see them. His wife is still with him."

June 10, 1944

"Boy has it ever been raining a lot today. I have written a couple letters and cleaned my BAR. It is a pretty good gun, but is heavy to carry. They shoot 20 times and you have to pull the trigger only once to do it. It is fully automatic."

"I'm glad to hear you have the beans and corn planted. The corn must be getting up pretty good if you can cultivate it."

"I'll bet the house really looks swell now since you have it all painted. It really is a swell home to have, and I wish that my shoes were under the bed right now. Ha, Ha."

June 19, 1944

"I saw Robert O'Neil today. We talked over old times, and about people back home."

"Mother, I read your letters over about 10 times before I even answer them."

"Say Mother, will you take some pictures of your flowers when they get in bloom? I would like to have some of them. You always had real pretty flowers before I left home. We never see any strawberries over here, but we have had pineapple three times a week since we landed here. I have eaten so many pineapples that the pineapple flies just about eat me up."

"We do have all of the ice cream, candy, gum and pop that we want over here. That's a lot of help."

June 21, 1944

"I am glad to hear that the corn is really growing now. You had pretty poor crops last fall and really need them this year."

"Harvey has painted that car about all the colors you can think of. Ask him if he wants some yellow paint? He really is a swell brother and son. I just hope that he can stay out of the army, for it will do him no good."

"I am glad the girls have a chance to go to Bible school, because that will do them a lot of good. We were in the field last week and that Sunday we had church on the hillside for an hour."

June 25, 1944

"I will drop you a couple lines this afternoon. It's Sunday when I really think of home. I often think what I would be doing if I was home right now."

"Boy, if I don't get home in another year I won't know anyone back there. I still get my Ionia County Newspaper and I can read about boys I know being home on furloughs anyway. It is nice to know all outfits aren't like this one. If we ever could get back I would have 45 days coming."

June 28, 1944

"I received your swell letter last night and was it ever good to hear from you again. I was on guard duty last night and all day today. It sure rained last night, but I didn't get wet."

"Those pictures were really OK. The one of you and Dad looked real good. You looked real young, and when I showed the boys, they wanted your address until I told them you were my mother. No kidding, it was really swell."

"Boy, are there ever a lot of mosquitoes over here now. It can rain here and be clear again in five minutes with the stars all out."

"The news is pretty good over the radio now. The war

could be over this year, but I hardly think so. It really should end in 1945 sometime."

July 1, 1944

"There hasn't much happened since I last wrote. We ran over about 10 mountains and had a parade today. I hate them worst of all. They gave some more Purple Hearts out, that is one reason we had it. Last week we had to swim 100 yards with our clothes on. That was pretty hard."

"Mother, yes I really wish my shoes were under the bed back home now. I have learned the ways of life the hard way."

"I was in San Francisco a year ago on the Fourth of July. That's Harvey's birthday too."

"Say I am going on a week's maneuvers starting tomorrow so I won't be writing this week. I sure don't like them. They are really harder than combat, but a lot safer."

"I was sorry to read about your chickens turning out so bad. I sure would like some of those fresh eggs you wrote about. We eat powdered eggs sometimes, and also powdered potatoes. I would like some good cold fresh milk also."

"I heard the Hit Parade on the radio tonight. They have a lot of good programs on Saturday night. I had a pint of ice cream too."

"Now just what do you think of the war? It gets harder every time over here. The news doesn't help much. It seems awfully slow to me."

"I still look at those pictures you sent me. They are really good. The house looks swell with the new paint too."

July 8, 1944

"I received your letter this week while we were on maneuvers, and it was really swell. I sure went over a lot of hills again, and was it ever hot out there. It rained almost every day too."

"I was sure glad to read where you have most of the hay up now. That is the hardest work we have at home."

"I have some Jap matchboxes which I will send home some day soon. Also I sent some pictures to Elrena a week

or so ago of Kwajalein, and she will send them on to you
sometime soon."

July 9, 1944

"Say Harvey, I have heard about you going to the dance
most every Saturday night. Can you dance yet? How does it
feel to be 18 years old now? You must think you are a man.
Ha, Ha. You should know how to swim pretty well by now
and also know a lot of those girls that always stay around
the lake."

"That car of yours must be the only one like that since you
painted it all those colors."

"Tell Mother that we weren't on the same island as the
marines at Kwajalein, but at the same atoll. You see there are
a lot of islands in one atoll, maybe thirty or forty, but the Japs
weren't on very many of them. We hit the largest island in
the atoll which was Kwajalein. They name the atoll after the
largest island."

"I hope we get some passes this week or I won't even know
how to get around town anymore. The last pass day I was on
guard duty and couldn't go."

July 1944

"Dad, I received your swell letter today and it sure was
good to hear from you again. It has been a long time since you
wrote a letter that long."

"I see you got the new grain drill, but will you get the
combine in time for the oats? The wheat must be ready to cut
by now."

"Did you get Harvey a B gas ration book? He needs one no
doubt. He has a lot of friends."

"I received six letters Sunday and five Monday. I never
saw a girl who could write so many swell letters."

"I don't know much about Dewey, but I would rather leave
it just as it is until after the war. The war is just going good
now and it would slow it up to change presidents now. That is
the way all the soldiers look at it too. I think that I will vote if
I can. I sent for a ballot anyway."

"You still have a lot of cows yet. I might not need those cows when I get home, as I have forgotten how to milk by now. Ha, Ha. I might not want to be a farmer now. When I left home that was what I wanted, but now I don't know what I want, and only time will tell."

"You are sure going on a lot of picnics lately. Well we have them too, but they are not near so much fun. Mother wrote that you won a prize. Good for you."

"What will those pheasants do this fall? I hope Robert gets a lot of them, but tell him I don't think he can shoot straight. Ha, Ha. I only hope that I can hunt just once more with Jake. He wouldn't know me now, I don't think. He must be about ten years old by now. Do you really think that he would still remember me yet?"
July 13, 1944

"Katherine, you can really write pretty good. A lot better than what I can. So you are in the 7th grade next year. It doesn't seem like you could be that far through school by now. You must be a big girl now that you are twelve years old."

"That Robert must be pretty big now. Do the girls still chase him or does he chase the girls now? I would bet even money that it is the last one."

"Say is that all the children that go to school now? The teacher shouldn't find it too hard to watch you with only twelve kids."

"Can you get those big brothers of yours to take you to the show? I would if I was home. I bet you and Mildred have a lot of fun together now that you are bigger. You did fight a lot when I was home, remember?"
July 13, 1944

"I was on a two-day pass and just came in last night. I saw some shows in town and Wednesday afternoon I saw Bob Hope and Francis Langford in person at Waikiki. There sure were a lot of soldiers and sailors out there."
July 15, 1944

"The name of the town I go most is Wahiawa. It isn't very far from camp, and it is easy to get there. There are buses that go there, but it is easier to catch a ride on a truck or jeep."

"Mother your house really looks swell. Everyone says it looks good from the outside, and if they could see the inside they would say the same thing. Those pictures of you and Dad really did look good to me."

"I have been on detail again today making packing boxes for the outfit. I was using a hammer and wore a blister on my hand, so you can see my hands are soft."

"The war should end before next year is over, and after this next action we might get a chance to come home. It sure would be nice to see it once more."

"We really had a poor supper tonight. Lately the food hasn't been very good. I weigh 186 pounds this week."

July 18, 1944

"Harvey I am glad you have all the first cutting hay up. You should have a lot more on the second cutting. How many acres of hay do you have in all?"

"Last Sunday I went down and saw Robert O'Neil. He was working that afternoon, but I wouldn't call it hard work. He had his telephone repair truck and we drove around the main post a lot. He has a swell job and will be here after the war is over. I don't think he will ever leave this island to go down under. I should have enlisted and got me a good job like that. I kid him about his job, and what he will tell folks about what he did in the war when he returns home."

"Say Harvey, you had better hope that you gave the right answer to all the questions they asked you. Don't think the army will make you tough either. I couldn't do half the work that I could before I came in the army. It doesn't build your arms up any. After about two years in the army you won't be any good for anything. Some of the things they do here are really crazy. There are two ways to do things. The army way and the right way, and we do it the army way. Dad really needs you more at home than what the army does."

"I hope you get the B ration book, as a boy with a girl friend really needs more gas. I guess you really need some better tires for your car. It would be a good car if you fixed the motor a little. I don't think that car has so many miles on it. You could fix a lot of it up yourself if you tried."

"You have a lot of bonds don't you? What are you going to do with all that money? You had better save it as after the war you will be able to use it. There will be some long cold days after the war. Just wait and see if I'm not right."

"Harvey, I will sell my half of the car for 25 dollars. You don't have to pay me until I get out of the army. I also will collect the 25 dollars on that insurance which I paid when you rolled my 39 over. In all it will only cost you 50 dollars and the car will be yours. Let me know if you want to do that."

July 20, 1944

"I couldn't write last night because we were out on maneuvers. I don't even feel much like writing tonight. My throat is a little sore and I have a cold. We only had about two hours sleep last night."

"Dad must be doing his share of fishing this summer. I would like to do a little of it myself. I have carried a gun so much since I came in the army that I might not like to hunt when I get out of here. We always take our guns with us whenever we go out and that is every day."

"I am glad you got a rain. We sure could use one here too. The dust is almost to the top of your shoes in some places. The trucks and tanks cut the roads up and then we get the dust. You have to take two showers a day and then you can't keep clean. It is that red dust too. I wouldn't live here if I had to spend the rest of my life on a boat. All the soldiers here won't ever come back once they get home, that's for sure."

"There will be a lot more boys missing before this war is over. It doesn't seem right that people would spend so much money to kill one another, when the same money would do them more good than what the war will. It wouldn't be so bad if it was over now, but it is only getting in high gear."

"Yes, those pictures from Kwajalein tell a sad story; I was on that airfield that's pictured and a few more places. The pictures were taken after the battle was over and there aren't any dead Japs shown. There were a lot of them before that though."

July 21, 1944

"Robert, so you can load hay now too, you must be pretty big. I still bet you and Harvey can't hold me down."

"You would like to have a car too, huh? What would you want with a bunch of junk, which that Ford was? You could have had it if Mother would have let you, but I don't think she would have."

"Say Robert, who is the girl you're sweet on? I write to about four or five myself, but only as a friend. Ha, Ha."

"Robert, are you going to do a lot of hunting this year? I bet that you still can't hit ducks like I could. Do you or Harvey ever clean my shotgun?"

July 26, 1944

"Yes Mother, we have cherry pie here once in awhile and I get my share if I can. Sometimes I get four or five pieces and put sugar and cream on them. We just don't have it very often. No, I never asked Elrena if she could bake a cherry pie. Do you think I should? Tell Dad that she has a job and her old man has a very big farm. I think her grandmother has some coins too. Ha, Ha. Don't let it worry you now. I still think she is a swell girl. Money doesn't worry me as much now as getting out of the army."

"I heard from Ralph Leland today, and he is in an anti-aircraft outfit. He hadn't shot any Jap planes down yet."

"The extra $10 per month is for infantry men only. It is for being in combat and doing OK. The dogfaces should get more money as we really do have a hard life. That is the best deal we have had yet. We really live in the ground when we're in combat. It is a long hard road with many hills in it. The infantry goes where everything else stops and it is tough at times. Most times! Ha, Ha."

"I am sure glad that Harvey won't have to go. You need him at home more than what we need him here. There isn't any future here in the army. That much I know. Next time I am going to be hard to find if I ever have to come back in the army, after I get out. There are a very few fellows who like it."

July 23, 1944

"I wouldn't care to be in the marines myself. I don't like the way they do things."

"So Clifton Miller is missing too? There are some boys here that have brothers missing and some that have been taken prisoner."

"Some guys sure are lucky to be home yet or at least in the states. Maybe they will let the older men that are overseas come home first when the war is over. They should do that much anyway."

August 1, 1944

"We had a big parade last week and President Roosevelt, General MacArthur and Admiral Nimitz were there to watch it. I couldn't see them very well as we walked by, but I could tell Roosevelt in his car. He looks pretty old, but just about like his pictures."

"I still have my radio and the news is pretty good. I hope it stays that way for the rest of the year."

"That new paint job on the house sure looks good and that grass looks good too. Over here the grass is all dead now. It is too hot and dry. They have the reddest dirt I've ever seen. Just looks like red clay back home. That is what they raise sugar cane and pineapples in. They have to irrigate all the land or it wouldn't be any good. The houses here wouldn't be good enough for our dog back home. It is always warm here so they don't need much, and that is just what they have, not much. Out near Waikiki there are some places that are pretty nice."

"I should go to the show tonight, but I don't get much fun out of them anymore. After you have been out all day you don't feel like going. There are always a lot of dogfaces and you can hardly find a seat. They do have some good ones and I don't miss many."

August 6, 1944

"I was on field maneuvers last week for three days and it wasn't any fun. We had a little sleep but not much. Friday night I never slept over two and a half hours. Last night I had a little more, but the ants ran all over me and I didn't like that a little bit."

"Went down to the main theater and saw a swell show. It was called Pin-Up Girl and Betty Grable was in it. She is a blonde and she also can sing."

"My radio still works and we have it on most of the time. It sure has been a lot of company to the boys here. Some of my friends even come over to hear it. When something important happens everyone is here."

August 9, 1944

"Mother, I haven't heard from you since a week ago last Friday which is almost two weeks. The mail is coming very slow, but I know you're writing."

"I just came in from a three-day pass and I saw my old buddy Snyder. I was over to his camp for two nights. He looks pretty good too. He is working in the PX now which is a good deal. We had a lot of fun together and I am going over to see them again next Sunday."

"I heard the news tonight a couple times. It sounds pretty good too. The war is winding down, but it will still take some time to end it, but that is still good news."

August 12, 1944

"Dad, I have had lots of mail this weekend. Now I will try to answer your swell letter."

"So you have a good water well now. I bet Harvey and Robert don't mind pumping the water now. Ha, Ha."

"I wish you would clean my shotgun up real good again then oil it and put it away. I don't want anyone using it either. The boys can use my rifle but my duck gun is a one-man gun and I want to keep it that way. I sure would give a lot to go hunting with Jake once more. If I get home on furlough and the season wasn't open, I'd still go a couple times for fun."

"I can see by those pictures that Mildred isn't the only one that has grown up since I left home. It looks like Harvey is bigger than you now, and when I come home I might have a little trouble showing him who's boss again, but I can do it. Katherine is almost as tall as Mother. Robert looks like a bull without horns. Does he still think he is as tough as he used to? It will seem funny when I get home as I still have them all in my mind as when I left, and they won't be that way."

"The President was on the radio tonight and I thought he gave a good talk. Most every soldier here feels like I do, that we should leave him in until after the war. Most soldiers also agree that the people back home wouldn't know there was a war going on if they didn't read it in the paper. The factory strikes back home aren't too popular with the boys here."
August 14, 1944

"Harvey, will you get to trap Bettinghouses's ponds this year? You had better get on the beam and get all the ponds you can. Hides should be worth more than last year, and after what you learned last year you should be able to do a lot better."

"I was sure glad to read that you got deferred until next year, Dad sure needs you a lot more than what the army does. Some of the other boys have had two or three deferrals so you should be able to stay out too."

"Guess you must have a girl friend now as you wrote that you were broke and owed Robert some money. With those new tires and B gas ration book you should be able to get around a little."

"You and Robert should be able to make some money with that new corn picker. I sure would like to be there and help you run it."
August 16, 1944

"I received a letter from Elrena last night. She didn't have much to say except how she was getting along with her work.

She is a swell girl, also they have a lot of oil and gas wells around her Dad's farm. Ha, Ha."

"I think it was better that I never got a furlough as it would have been hard to come back to this old army life after being home a couple weeks. Some of the boys who had them said it wasn't as much fun as it sounded. They even came back a couple days early."

"I sent home a grass skirt for the girls this week, and it is for both of them. They can put it on up in their room or do whatever they want with it. I couldn't see much use in buying two of them."

August 19, 1944

"Tell Robert thanks for oiling my gun up. I kind of miss that duck hunting back home. Tell him I got a watch for him today, a Bulova 15 jewels for three dollars. It might not be too good either."

"You should know who a dogface is. That is what they call us mudslingers."

"So your cousin got married. I thought he was over here. That is what makes a lot of boys mad, seeing some boys who have been in the states two and three years. They should change them with us, but I don't ever look for that to happen. I will still be here yet at the end of the war, which isn't as close as most people think. It will still be a Christmas or two before we get out. No doubt you wouldn't like me anyway and chase me out before one weekend had gone by. For I have really changed a lot. Well if you did I would have to go out to Kansas to live. Ha, Ha."

"It does seem funny, because when I came in the army I knew just what I wanted to do when I got home, but now I don't. We won't worry about it now until the time comes."

"I went to the show last night, but it wasn't very good. They are having a stage show tonight, but it is still the same old thing. I have a lot of letters to answer tonight, and I would rather write letters than go to a show."

August 21, 1944

"I received a letter from Ralph Leland today. He is on Saipan. He says the army is just the same as always, once the Japs were killed. He said he could do as much back in the states as he is doing there and save the government the twenty percent overseas pay."

"Yesterday I saw O'Neil and we had a big talk. He gets the daily hometown paper so we had a lot of them to read. We read about some dogfaces home on furlough and that gave us something to gripe about for a half hour."

September 4, 1944

"I see by your letters that you and Dad took a trip. Yes, I did forget Dad's birthday. Guess I had too much on my mind about other things."

"Say, Katherine must be a pretty good cook by now. When I get home I want her to cook me a big dinner all by herself, and I hope it won't be too long either."

"That new 40 acres should be good land, but it will cost a lot to get much back from it."

September 5, 1944

"Harvey, I received three of your letters, but haven't been able to answer them. I just couldn't write until last night when I wrote Mother a letter."

"There should be a lot of cordwood on that 40 acres you bought. It takes a lot of wood to make a hundred cords doesn't it? Ha, Ha."

"Say Harvey, do you remember the big watermelon we got that one day when Mitchell was along? I still have to laugh over it."

"I guess Earl Presscott saw a lot of action. Was he hit by a bullet or shrapnel? I guess you can see that war is no fun, so you had better stay out of it if you can. It isn't like hunting ducks or rabbits. The bullets aren't so bad, but when the big shells start coming in and shrapnel starts flying around your hole it is time to call the whole thing off. Once it came pretty close to our hole and we really pulled our tails into it."

September 6, 1944

"I went through the Dole Pineapple Factory in Honolulu. It is pretty big and covers 43 acres in all. They have girls to take you through in bunches of 10 or 12."

"Yes, all the boys who have the medal get the extra 10 dollars per month. I don't think the marines get it, only the infantry. I don't know the reason why some of the boys didn't get the medal, but I heard it was because they weren't up on the front when they should have been."

"Last Monday night the boy who was next to me in the hospital ward came down to see me. He just came back from a 30-day furlough at home. I never knew him before the hospital, but now we are good friends."

"So you think the best place for me would be on a farm? Well I still like farming and whatever I do I always want a farm as a sideline, but I can name a lot better ways to make a living. I would still like to get Uncle Albert's business in San Francisco if he wants to sell out when the war is over."

September 9, 1944

"Dad I received your swell letter this last week and it is the nicest letter you ever wrote me. It was real swell."

"I am sure glad that your corn is good this year as you stand a good chance to make some money on it."

"I went to Honolulu today on a pass, and it was a pretty good day. I had fried oysters with cold tea and pie with ice cream. I went to the show today and saw a couple of the old boys. We had a good time after that."

"I have my ballot here now, so I will have to send it in pretty soon. I won't tell you how I voted. It's a secret to every-one. Ha, Ha."

September 10, 1944

"I played cards last night until two this morning, and I didn't do myself any good either. I didn't lose much so it wasn't so bad. My luck has been poor this last month."

"I sure could use some more sleep today. I can hardly write this letter. When you write Elrena that letter you better put a good word in for me."

September 24, 1944

"So your gas gave out? Ha, Ha. Well Harvey, you will have to walk as I do."

"So you have watermelons now. I wish I could get into them."

"Say brother if you sell the car, half of what you get is mine. Get all you can cause it makes me more."

"If I have any shells for a 20 gauge shotgun, you and Robert can have them, half and half. Can you buy shells now? If you can't tell Dad to use my 12 gauge, but clean it and put it back when he's done. I don't want some poor shot shooting it while I am gone. They might spoil it for me. Someone like my two brothers."

September 28, 1944

"I was on KP today, and it was easy. We eat very good here. I had some ice cream here too, and was it ever good."

"I have your girl's picture here, and everyone that saw it thought she was pretty swell. How many other ones have you?"

"Say Harvey, how is Jake this year for hunting?"

October 3, 1944

"I had forgotten all about Labor Day until I saw it in your letter. It wasn't long after that, in '42, that I went in the army. That was a sad day, but I didn't know it at the time. We all thought that the war would be over in a year or so. I can still remember the train leaving Ionia that day."

"Boy, I would sure like to get into some of that pie you make. I miss that food from the garden most. We don't get any green food since we've been overseas. It would taste a lot better if you were cooking it too."

"About the farm of Ora's. I don't want it myself, but Harvey is doing the work and helping so you should do what he wants. I don't think I want a farm when I come home. I have some other ideas on my mind right now. Use some of Harvey's ideas as he will have some good ones. Harvey will feel the same way too."

October 6, 1944

"Dad, I received your letter today and I sure was glad to hear from you. Duck hunting must be good there. I received your pictures and will keep them. I don't know much about that farm of Myers, but I would like land a little closer to home if I was you. Do what you want to do. I am in the army and might not want to farm when I get out. Who knows what the future will hold for us?"

"I don't know the Conklin girl, but give her my address and I might. Ha, Ha. Is she the oldest, or her sister?"

"They are having a show in camp tonight, so I am going. I will have tomorrow off and write Mother a letter."

October 1944

"I can write you now that I am aboard a ship. That is the reason my letters have been far apart."

"Say I would sure like to have some of those oysters that you can fix. It won't be long until I will have a birthday and then Dad can have my oysters."

"By this time you shouldn't miss my letters very much. The best thing you could do would be to forget all about me and save yourself a lot of worrying. I never did near as much for you as what you have for me. You and Dad have done a lot for me as I can see after talking to other boys. I don't know if I will be able to live at home or not after the war. I kind of hate to go home and have all those people asking me the same questions over all the time, and I know they will. Maybe after it is over I will feel different. It won't ever seem like the home I left in '42."

"I bet Dad sure hated to have the boys get more ducks than he. Robert must be a pretty good shot now. They will be hunting pheasants soon, so Dad can catch up. Old Jake will be right there I bet. He should be better now, than when he was young. Shouldn't be so fast and not so crazy."

"I have a wonderful suntan. We have some short pants and I wear mine on the deck. The sun is really hot reflecting off the water and so bright you have to wear sunglasses most of the time."

"I still get my share of letters from Elrena. She sends half of the mail I get. Sometimes she writes in the morning and then again at night. She wrote that her brother said he wasn't going to work home another winter and her Dad said if he didn't he would sell the farm."

"I sent home all my pictures, but a couple which I have in my billfold. I still have the same one you sent me for Christmas almost two years ago. It will be the one I hope to take out of the army too. It is in good shape yet. It was with me all the time since I left the USA, even the time I was in that duck that went down in the ocean."

"Now I will close for this time and don't worry too much about me for I will be all right."

Leyte

We left Hawaii on the USS Golden City. Before the war it had been a passenger liner, so it had nice accommodations. There was a swimming pool but it was empty and painted a drab color. They also had the capability to make ice cream which sure suited me just fine. The Golden City was to be our home for quite awhile, as there didn't seem to be much of a rush to go anywhere.

At Eniwetok Island we had time to swim and relax. I looked for rocks they call cat eyes, but could only find a couple poor ones. Most of the time though, life on the troopship was boring. There was no entertainment, and much of our time was spent in line for the two meals a day. In between the meals the platoon sergeant held an exercise session. We stayed up on deck most of the time because it was so hot below.

When a thousand men lined up for a meal the line went all around the deck and it was some time before you got to the food which was below deck. I supplemented the two meals with a third one when I could. The navy fed us, but the army provided their cooks to help out. I watched the routine and when the army cooks went in early to eat, I just walked in with them, filled a plate and hid out on deck someplace to eat. Nobody said anything and I just acted as if I owned the place. One day a guy in the squad saw me eating and asked how I got the food. I said to just walk in and get some, but when he tried it they kicked him out. Later, I went in and got another plate of food and gave it to the guy.

On the First of October, the normal ship routine was interrupted when we crossed the equator. That was kind of a wild time for the sailors aboard who hadn't done it before. They were treated to a real mean initiation. Before the crossing they were called pollywogs, and something different afterwards. With their head and arms in a rack, the other guys would hit them in the ass with a paddle and pour red dye on them. Some would try to hide and avoid the punishment, but they'd usually get caught and in the process get their clothes ripped off. None of us had been across, but they didn't do anything to us except give us a certificate.

At first we heard we were headed for Truk Island, and then the decision was made to bypass the Japs there, and head on to the Philippines. Our attack was to be Leyte Island.

It had been 38 days since we had left Hawaii, and soon the peaceful cruise would end in a not so peaceful place. We had a lot of company though, as there were ships all around us.

In a briefing room they had a big table set up with a model of the island. Roads, airfields and beach outlines were shown along with where each unit would be landing and the positions where they would initially move to. Left out were the Jap strongholds, which they either weren't sure of, or didn't want to tell us.

Our company was to be held in reserve, so on the 20th of October we were the last to leave the ships, after everyone else had landed. We moved up on the beach about 200 yards, and dug in. The Japs seemed to be gone as there were none to greet us. That afternoon we just sat around and talked, listened to some fighting in the distance and figured we had a good deal being in reserve.

About 10 o'clock that evening our good deal ended. We were told to prepare to move in 10 minutes. I had my pack cut down pretty good now, so my load was light and it didn't take me long to get ready. Soon we were on our way up this road which headed straight into the island. We didn't know where we were going or why, but as we moved up the road, two men abreast, the Jap shells started working towards us. There was a ditch on each side of the road and when we heard a shell coming in we'd dive for the nearest one. We didn't find out the big picture until the next day, but what had happened was that our regiment, the 184th, was on the left side of the road and had moved up faster and dug in well ahead of the 32nd regiment which was on the right side of the road. This left a large area where the Japs could come across in front of the 32nd and get behind the 184th. I don't know when they discovered this weak area, but it must have been late otherwise we'd have been moved in earlier. They had us spread out along the quarter mile gap taking positions facing the road on the left side. It was dark and difficult to figure out what was going on as we were facing the road and the fighting was taking place up the road to our left. We started to dig in, and the fighting at the front seemed to be getting worse.

We had only been there about 30 minutes when two jeeps came speeding down the road toward us with their little blackout lights on. We then heard a clattering noise coming, and when we first realized they were tanks we thought they might be ours. When they started shooting we knew they were Japs. The tanks passed so close I could have reached out and touched them with a bayonet. The lead tank had its big gun aimed as low as possible. It was a 47mm, or something like that, and when they fired it, there was a seven foot ball of fire from its blast. They knew we were along the road and figured they would get us with the shrapnel. A Jap was up on the tank turret and leaned over and sprayed the first platoon with machine gunfire. It was as if he knew exactly where to shoot. He wounded 10 but didn't kill any. I guess his clip was empty when he went by us, cause he didn't shoot. The guy in the hole with me wanted to get out and run, but I convinced him he'd get shot by our guys if he was out of his hole.

The tanks headed down to the beach, but it got too hot for them there so they came back towards us. Before they left the beach area, the boys there got one tank and the 32nd strong point got another. When we heard the last tank coming back our way there was no question as to whether it was friend or foe. The tracers hitting the tank looked like a swarm of fireflies. Of course the rifle and machine gun bullets didn't hurt the tank but we had a bazooka loaded and ready for him. A guy close to me in our platoon put a bazooka shell right through the armor and caught the tank on fire. The tank was just a little to my left when it got hit.

A Jap jumped out of the tank with a grenade, but he was caught in a hail of bullets and was dead by the time he hit the ground.

That night we expected the Jap infantry to come through our positions shortly after the tanks. I was really scared. It was the only time that I ever remember my teeth chattering. I could just imagine 1000 Japs coming down that road. Our artillery pounded the road beyond us anticipating an attack, but to our surprise no Jap infantry came. It's a good thing, because we weren't dug in good and ready to fight. I guess they had different tactics in mind and the tanks were operating alone, but I think they made a mistake not pressing the attack. We should have known on the first pass the tanks weren't ours, because ours aren't as noisy, and they're not dumb enough to be out at night. In fact our tanks seemed to work 8 hours a day and I thought sometimes they had weekends off too.

The next morning I could see the Jap that jumped out of the tank was an officer. He had a big wide leather belt with a shoulder strap and regular leggin's. He still had the grenade in his hand. The pin had been pulled, but he didn't have a chance to hit it on something hard to start the fuse.

As we moved toward the front the next morning I could see the damage the Japs had done. Our regiment had a 57mm antitank gun set up on the road, and the Japs had run right over it with a tank. The metal shield around the barrel was flattened. The antitank boys had knocked out a tank there, but a lot of Americans had been killed and some still laid on the ground. The rest had been in the jeeps that went by us. The tank we hit was the only one that burned.

Our lieutenant had always said if you were fighting tanks the place to be was right behind them cause they couldn't get you there. Well I looked at that Jap tank and right out the back about 18 inches off the ground was a machine gun. The guy inside would have almost had to lay on his belly to fire it, but if you'd have been behind that tank they would have probably called you shorty for the rest of your life.

We moved up all that next day but things weren't too bad. We'd pick off a few now and then, however the Japs had room to back up and set up new lines.

Just before dark my squad was picked to put an outpost out 2000 yards in front of our lines. This was supposed to be a listening outpost to warn the rest if the Japs were coming. With only 10 men we were not supposed to fight, just watch and if it got too rough, everyone for himself. The guy with me and I decided we'd try and stick together if that happened. In each hole we had two men facing opposite directions, and in one hole we had the aid man and sergeant with a phone between the two men. That was a real long night. At one time we had about 10 to 15 Japs walk right by us. We were about ready to open up on them but didn't. Boy, I was glad of that. It was scary as you could see their bayonets in the moonlight.

The next day our colonel found out about our assignment and he said no more of that. We really couldn't have done any good out there anyway. If the Japs were really coming they would find out soon enough. That was one order the colonel gave that I liked.

The Japs had a lot more airplanes than we did, and they were around overhead quite a bit. They didn't usually bother with soldiers, but if they spotted any of our trucks on the road they would roll in and try to shoot them up. This one day a truck was coming down the road and some Jap planes spotted him and started to attack. We couldn't see them very well because of the trees, but we heard them coming and made good time to holes, ditches, whatever was available for cover. After they made a firing pass they would cut off to the side real fast to avoid being a good target themselves, and when they did we could see the pilots sitting in there. We all opened fire when they went past, but they were hard to hit because you had to lead them a lot. Well this one guy went by and I gave him about 20 rounds out of the BAR. I think we might have hit him because after that pass they left, popping over the mountain, and he just ran into it. There was no smoke from the plane, so we figured we hit the pilot.

We sent a tank up the road ahead of the troops on kind of a recon mission, but that didn't work too well. He found the Japs all right, but the road was so narrow and muddy that he had a hard time turning around to get out of there. Before he did get turned around the Japs had hit the tank 10 times. Fortunately they were only aiming at the turret. The shells put three-inch-deep gouges in the thick metal but didn't stop him from getting away. If they would have aimed at the tracks or a more vulnerable spot, he would have been a goner. That ended the single tank recon patrols.

The road from the beach went in towards the center of the island about 12 miles and ended at a small village. We pushed the Japs that far and then they fell back into the hills and mountains. In the village there were a lot of grass huts and a schoolhouse with a tin roof that probably had been built by Americans. The schoolhouse had several bags of Jap rice and piles of shoes stored in it, and this we let the Filipinos have. Those little people could throw a 100 pound bag of rice on their back and take off with it for miles and never set it down. I don't know how they did it.

That night we set up our positions in town at the end of the road. We formed our own strong point in kind of a circle, for you never knew for sure which way the Japs would come from. They set the machine gun where the main road had ended and had it in a horseshoe-shaped dugout. The gun could be swung in an arc to cover both the road and a path that ran perpendicular to it. I was in the first hole to the left and the first platoon was dug in along the path in the opposite direction.

Well it was pretty dark out when along the path came this Jap on a bicycle. He didn't know that we held that ground, but he surprised us too. In fact when the machine gun boys saw him and started firing he was so close and their gun dug in so low, that they just blasted away his wheels. The Jap tumbled right into their hole. The Jap was as surprised as the boys in the hole were, and he didn't know what to do at first, but managed to get out of there before they could get him. He ran off past a line of guys and right over the top of at least four of the 1st platoon foxholes. Everybody was firing now, but it was pretty dark and the Jap was moving fast until he got caught in some barbwire. I don't know how he did it, but he got untangled and got away. With all of that shootin' in all directions, it's a wonder some of our guys didn't shoot each other.

The next morning everybody was talking about the Jap on the bicycle. The machine gun boys were all cleaning their pistols, cause when the Jap fell in their hole none of the pistols would fire. Too much dirt in the mechanisms I guess. There was this young guy they called Fuzz, because he never shaved. He had been complaining lately that he hadn't had a chance to kill a Jap yet. I said, "Fuzz, why didn't you shoot that Jap last night? He came right by you." Disgustingly he replied, "Yeah, he went right over the top of my hole and I couldn't hit him."

While we were chasing the Japs toward the mountains, things took a turn for the worse in the Gulf of Leyte. The navy had brought along three small aircraft carriers to provide some air cover for the invasion, and they were operating in the gulf. I guess the navy thought things were pretty secure there, because they pulled their warships out and were chasing the Jap navy north of the islands. Someplace the Japs had been hiding some cruisers, and after the main navy force had left the gulf the Japs brought their cruisers around the south end of the island and sunk the three aircraft carriers. They didn't hang around to inflict any additional damage, but now the Jap aircraft operating from other islands had free rein to work us over. Plus, they attacked our ammunition dump and supplies on the beachhead.

After a couple days on the island we received word about the loss of our air support and that the only mortar shells we would have were the ones we were carrying. The Japs had destroyed the rest.

For over a week we had been head to head with the Japs, but now we might go two days and not see any. It was gonna be a tough fight chasing them through the hills. The Japs were part of the 24th Division and had already beat the Americans the first time. We didn't figure they would be scared of us this time. As it turned out they decided to put us back on reserve. We were trucked back down to the beach to help unload supplies the navy brought in.

What a mess it was around the beach. The Japs had destroyed a lot of stuff and it was the rainy season too. There was a rain downpour most every night and by morning it was a muddy mess. We helped the navy unload ammunition and supplies for a couple of days and got some warm food. I remember the navy gave us a whole bunch of bread that had mold on it, but with butter it sure tasted good. We ate it all up. It would be the last bread we'd see for at least two months.

A road followed the coast along the south end of the island and crossed the mountains. We headed down the road with the trucks, but because of the rain each night the trucks were always getting stuck and making ruts in the red clay. It was funny though, when the sun did come out it was so hot, that by afternoon the trucks would be stirring up dust.

There didn't seem to be many Japs on the east side of the mountains, but we did see Filipinos along the road, and one bunch had a fire going. They were cooking something and as we approached they came up to the trucks and offered us some baked bananas. It was kind of a cool rainy day and the bananas really tasted good.

November 1944

"It has been a long time since you have heard from me, so I hope you will enjoy this. I am back in the war again, but I am OK. I am on a Philippine island and it rains every day. It is really hot between showers too. My feet are wet all the time with mud all over my shoes. I go across rivers with my clothes on to get the mud out of them. I haven't received any mail in a long time. Maybe I will get some soon. So far I haven't had it very bad. I haven't shot my rifle since we landed. I was on patrol this morning, but never saw any Japs. I have seen lots of native people. They are around all the time."

As the road crossed the mountains at the south end of the island, we started to see a lot more activity than we had seen for several days. To begin with, our fighters were starting to use the two Jap airfields that had been captured on the east side of the mountains. We could watch the dog fights between the Japs and our boys, and saw some of their pilots and some of ours get shot down. The navy had a bunch of ships on the west side of the island and the Japs were intent on attacking them. Some of the Jap pilots would fly their planes right into the side of a ship and blow it up. We could see our boys jumping off the ships as they went down, and some made it to shore. Unfortunately we were not in a good position to help them.

On the west side of the mountains things got a lot worse for us. The road crossed a lot of rivers and small streams, and most of the bridges had been blown up, so the trucks couldn't go any farther. Also we were back in contact with the Japs. The heat was really hard on us too. Even though we had come from Hawaii which had a warm climate, it was much worse here. I remember guys just passing out walking down the road. They had to be carted off to an aid station. Finally, the sergeant made sure everyone took his salt tablets and that seemed to help a lot.

It was hard for the supplies to keep up with us now. Getting the wounded out was the first priority and getting the ammunition in was the second. Our food supply was really short. The same thing happened at Kwajalein. It seemed like the army didn't consider that a high priority for the soldiers in combat.

We captured two airfields. The first didn't look like a very good one, but I think they intended it to look that way. Two guys drove a jeep over some bombs the Japs had buried there and it blew the jeep to pieces and killed both of them. The next airfield looked really good. There was all kinds of US equipment that the Japs had captured when they first took the island. The Japs had driven our army trucks so long that the tires were about gone. There were Atlas batteries and tires, turning lathes and even a bunch of Red Cross supplies. They had our coke bottles mounted on trees as telephone line insulators. I think the stuff they had captured from us when they first took the island really helped them make it rough for us. They might have had a tough time surviving if they hadn't had it.

At the second airport the Japs had fixed up a bunch of revetments with dummy airplanes in them. From the ground the fake airplanes didn't look like much. They had poles propping up the wings and they were just made of scrap stuff. From the air they must have looked pretty realistic, for you could see our pilots had machine-gunned and bombed them pretty good. The whole object of this airfield was to take the pressure off the other airfield which they were using.

I found a Jap magazine laying outdoors at the good airfield. It had been out in the rain for some time, so I tried to dry it out to save it. There were lots of photos in it showing captured Americans and their equipment, along with our airplanes they had shot down. The magazine showed the victorious Japanese beside their flag and their commanders all happy with their success. I bet now they would have a little trouble looking so happy. Later I mailed it home, and was surprised it made it through the censors intact.

We were seeing a lot more Japs now. I don't know if they were left over from the airfield or not, but there were plenty of them. They could cause us some real problems if they felt like it, and that made us a little scared.

This one night we were all in our three-man foxholes when word came down that there were 100 Japs near our positions. There was no official password used on the front, we were just told to remain in our foxholes until morning, and everyone understood what that meant. My squad sergeant passed the word to the next squad and then he saw someone out in front of our lines. He said, "Halt!" The thing ducked down and he shot. The thing had been a man from the 3rd squad, and he was dead. The sergeant was never right after that.

For the rest of that night we were on double alert. That is when everyone watches and no one sleeps. We had two other men in our company shot that way. One was hit twice by a BAR, right in the butt. The bullets went right through the cheeks of his ass making eight holes, four in each cheek. He didn't sit down again for a long time. The other guy was hit in the head on Kwajalein, and lived, but never was right after that.

November 1944

"I haven't had a letter from you since the 12th of September, but they should be coming soon."

"I am OK and eating every day, but only two meals and some days only one. We don't have much time some days. We have ten in one rations and they are good. We heat them if we have time."

"We have lots of patrols to go on. We sure have a lot of rain here and we have to walk in mud and water most of the time. It rained all day yesterday and last night too."

"I took a bath in the river today and shaved too. The water is cool and we sure enjoy it when we can get in. I go in with my clothes on most of the time to get the mud off."

"They have more ants and bugs on this island than in the whole USA. There are lots of mosquitoes too, the kind that cause malaria fever. I almost forgot the flies, but they are here too."

"I have lots of souvenirs, including the money the Japs use on the Philippines, and one Jap dog tag. Also a book with lots of pictures of the fighting when the Japs first took the islands.

I am sending some of the money home in this letter, but it is worthless I guess."

"We have very little news here, but now they have a little paper which is printed here on the island. I heard about the president going back in office again. I guess that isn't what you wanted is it?"

"I have really been eating the coconuts here, they have some kind of drink here they make out of coconut milk which tastes like hard cider, but it kicks the hell out of you."

"I am 24 years old. I went on patrol the day of my birthday."

November 17, 1944

"It is raining today, as most every day. I was on patrol all day yesterday and when we got in I went swimming. On the patrol we crossed a couple of rains. That was almost the same as swimming. You can't go anywhere here without getting all wet."

"I see where you and Dad have been married 25 years. I guess you and Dad have had as happy a life as anyone could have. I hope so anyway. I have been around a little myself and I can see and say that our family gets along the best and did more for each other than 99 out of 100. We can all see how it has paid off in the end. There isn't a one of us kids that shouldn't be very proud of our home. I know I am."

"I know that I am not sorry that I worked at home those five years. At the time they didn't seem important at all, but now you think of them and they seem like a vacation. I don't know how to express it but I will always remember them as the best of my life."

"Tell Mildred that I appreciate very much that she blew my birthday candles out. I couldn't have picked out anyone else that I would rather have do it."

"That picture of the corn really looks good to me. The boys all said it makes them homesick. They raise corn here which looks like popcorn. They don't take care of it. All they do is plant it and from then on it is up to the corn."

November 19, 1944

"Well I am OK and swimming every day. We eat pretty good now, with B rations. They are cooked for us by the cook. Ten in one, and C rations we cook ourselves."

"I have a swell souvenir from the Philippines, if I ever get it home. It is a handmade bola knife. I never saw anything like it before."

"When I get home I don't want to rest for six months. I would like to get to work within a week or so because if I don't I will have too much time on my hands."

After the airfields we had some pretty easy duty for a change. There was a good-sized bridge that was still intact, and we were assigned guard duty there. I guess they figured it might be valuable enough to us in the future that they didn't want the Japs coming in and blowing it up. We used 10 men to guard the bridge, in a five-man shift. There was a pretty good-sized river there and it was fun watching the Filipinos fishing. They would bend over in the shallow water so that only their butt stuck up, and with a single-tine spear they would spear these four-inch fish. I don't know how they did it, but they were pretty good. Also with a net they would gather crabs and dump them in a basket. This stuff would eventually all wind up cooking together in a big kettle. The Filipinos would usually offer us some of their food, but we were told not to eat it, because our bodies couldn't stand all the germs, but theirs could. I never did eat any of it cause I didn't think a lot of those people looked too healthy. They had sores on their legs and under the skin they had lumps, where ulcers had healed, the size of a hazelnut. Lots of things were available to take your health, hookworms, malaria and elephant fever. The mosquitoes didn't seem too bad though, and that was surprising. I didn't even see any snakes, though there were supposed to be a couple of real poisonous varieties around.

There were lots of water buffalo, and with the big horns they looked threatening. They were pretty slow though, and you could see little kids leading them around. They used them to plow and do other chores, but sometimes the water buffalo would walk into a small pond to cool themselves and then the Filipinos had a heck of a time getting them out.

The Filipinos would come up to us and trade eggs and things for our food. One man had a hundred eggs all numbered with a pencil from one to a hundred and I traded something for 50 of them. The eggs were all mixed together, but he still carefully sorted out the eggs numbered one through 50. I still don't know why he had them numbered other than that was the order they were laid in, and he wanted to sell the oldest. Well they were good, and the five guys on my shift all had a big egg feast.

November 1944

"I received three letters from you since I wrote last. I got those pictures of Katherine, Mildred and Robert. That grass skirt doesn't look too hot to me. Maybe if the right girl had it on it would look better. Ha, Ha."

"I haven't received a letter from Elrena yet. Maybe she is giving me the run-around or maybe she thinks I am the one doing that. I still bet she has 40 letters in the mail somewhere."

"I went swimming this afternoon and had some fun. The civilians stand around and watch us swim like they never saw a white man before. There are some nice looking girls here, but don't worry they still look pretty bad yet."

"We eat chicken a lot when we can trade them out of it. Also lots of bananas. If you have one candy bar they will work for you. They have gone to school so they are not as dumb as they look."

"I will send you some more of that Jap money. I have lots of it."

November 1944

"I went swimming two times today and wrote Elrena a letter. I received five letters from her two days ago and four today. I received two from you Mother, and the picture of the seed corn was in it."

"Yes I would have liked to hunt some of those pheasants this year, but I couldn't. How does old Jake work this year?"

"I was so close to three Jap tanks that I could have written my name on the side. I just let them go on by. I also shot 20 times at an airplane, but I no doubt missed it. I saw a Jap plane shot down a couple days ago."

"My mail is all mixed up. I get old mail and some that I call new mail, but it is three weeks old already. It is still mail and that is all right with me."

"Say, how did my birthday cake taste anyway? Did you have oysters too?"

"What do you think of Dewey now? I knew from the first he would never make it. Soldiers are almost 100 percent for Roosevelt, and I can see why too."

"I pulled guard duty last night from 9 to 11 and 3 to 5 this morning. That kind of hurts my sleep a little every night, but we get by."

"It is pretty hot here in the daytime and rains most every night. They say the rain season hasn't started yet, and that is what worries me most."

Not too long after we had captured the airfields our air force started using one of them. Things were in full swing when one night the Japs dropped in a bunch of paratroopers and retook most of the field. The airfield was protected by antiaircraft guns and numerous sandbagged positions, but when the Japs dropped in, the air defense units on one side of the field abandoned their positions and ran over to join those on the other side. That gave the Japs half the airfield. Part of our company was dispatched back up there to retake the airfield, but not before the Japs had destroyed all the airplanes there.

On Thanksgiving Day we were still guarding this bridge when a jeep pulled up. A GI inside handed us two old chickens and we asked him what we were supposed to do with them. He said he didn't care, but President Roosevelt said that everyone was gonna have chicken for Thanksgiving, and here were ours. We had a little gas stove and a one quart pan to put them in, so the other five-man shift cooked theirs all afternoon. When they were through we cooked ours until 10 that night and then pulled it apart so we all could have a little. Actually the only thing that was any good was the juice it had cooked in. We had added bouillon powder to the juice as it cooked, and that made it quite tasty. I guess the president was satisfied that we got our chickens, but it was not a good deal, and it would have been better to have some clean socks.

Every so often the Filipinos would roast a pig and give us some. The pigs weren't very big, about the size of a woodchuck, so there wasn't a lot to go around. They were good though. I asked the Filipinos what they would do if the Japs came back, and they indicated that they would head for the hills. We didn't have a lot of trust for them, and the longer we were there the less trust we had. Our worry was who's side they would be on when things got tough.

While we were at the bridge they shipped our duffle bags up so we had a change of clothes. That would be the last time I would see my duffle bag, and the last change of clothes until January. The clean clothes felt good and we were well rested and reasonably healthy too. They had even brought water up for us.

It was fun to watch the Filipino kids jumping off the bridge. I think they learned to swim before they could walk. Some only looked like they were five years old. When they swam, they looked like little bullfrogs in the water.

Somehow from coconuts, the Filipinos made a drink that was like hard cider. They would use a chunk of bamboo pole as a bottle to hold it and some shredded hemp as a top. For a peso you could buy some, and enough could make you drunk. I watched a Filipino washing out his bamboo jugs in the river. I guess he figured his legs were dirty, cause he took the hemp bottle top to sponge off his legs. That cured me from drinking any more of his coconut juice.

While we were guarding bridges the 32nd had been moving ahead doing the fighting. They were in trouble now, and had been pushed back a couple of miles. What had happened was that the Japs had sent some troopships over and we saw them offshore and wondered why they weren't being fired upon. I can't say if it's true for sure, but what we heard happened was that our commanders figured the troopships were there to evacuate the Japs off the island. Their plan was to wait until the ships were loaded and then shell hell out of them. That was not the Jap plan. At night they unloaded a whole bunch of fresh troops that were ready to fight, and they were really causing the 32nd problems.

We hadn't fought for quite awhile so we were told we'd have to move up to the front. In the morning we walked up to the small village of Bay Bay. There weren't many people there, just a few of those split bamboo houses lined the street. They were built on poles about three feet off the ground and would hold about 10 people. In about two days they could build one. The men would cut the poles with bolo knives and set the stakes and tie the joints. The women wove grass for the roof.

Arriving early we had the whole day to kill before we moved up to relieve the 32nd. Our unit chaplain, whom we called Padre, was wandering around and somehow he scared up a Jap. The Jap had a bayonet and started chasing the Padre. My buddy was a headquarters guard, and not too far away when he saw the Jap chasing Padre. The Padre was yelling, "Shoot him, Shoot him!", and my buddy did. The chaplain was a nice guy, but we got a kick out of the fact that instead of waving the good book at the Jap, he had called for the gun.

My second scout was called Saki Joe, because everywhere he went he was always checking every bottle the Japs left behind to see if he could find some alcohol to drink. Well Joe and a couple other guys found some rice whiskey somewhere and really got happy. In fact they were so bad they could hardly walk. The sergeant was really mad. There was a water tank with spring water that we ducked their heads into, then walked them around for awhile and ducked their heads in again. Every time we walked them by the sergeant they would say, "Hi sarge", and that made him madder. It didn't seem right that we had to take care of these guys, cause we hadn't been drinking. I guess the sergeant thought we should be responsible for them. We finally got them sobered up and that night we moved up behind the 32nd and took over their positions just before daylight.

The hole that I was to have was on the side of a hill and I said to the boys leaving it, "This doesn't look so bad." "Wait till night, you'll see. It gets bad," they replied. I could see some Japs laying around, and that they'd had a little problem.

We were using three-man foxholes, and they were the best. One guy would sleep while the other two watched in opposite directions.

We worked all day hauling ammunition 1000 yards uphill to the holes, but during that time we still had one or two men always watching in each hole. Just before dark we were out setting up some barbwire in front of our hole when a shot rang out and a Texas boy on the other end of the wire was shot in the chest and died in a few minutes. I was next to him with a pole through the wire. I quit running the barbwire and noticed our third man was missing. I found him down in the hole underneath our ponchos, and he was scared so bad he never was any good after that. I couldn't make him sit up and look out at all that night. He had shakes and fits so bad the medics finally took him back, and I heard later they made a truck driver out of him.

There was a hill that separated us from another company and we needed that to close our lines. It was called Bamboo Ridge, and boy was it hard to take. We would shoot all kinds of mortar shells up there and then take off up the hill to where you could almost see the top. At that point all hell broke loose. A lot of guys were getting shot and you couldn't see anything, so we pulled back. The next day they tried the same thing with a different platoon, but without success. That went on for five days before we would take the ridge. In between attacks we had to haul ammunition and mortar shells on our back up the hill, and that was hard work. After one fifteen minute mortar barrage on the hill the lieutenant who was in command said, "There goes another 45,000 dollars. Probably 50 Japs and a few machine guns up there." The top of the hill was covered with smoke and dust. It was hard to see how anything up there could live.

We finally took the hill, and the bamboo on top looked like toothpicks. The lieutenant was wrong, because later they figured there had been 300 Japs and 20 to 30 machine guns. Also, these were the fresh Jap troops that had been recently unloaded and they were ready for a good fight. The 1st platoon lieutenant was one of those killed on the hill.

I noticed that during those five days we were trying to take Bamboo Ridge, two of our machine guns that covered each attack had accumulated a truckload of shells. You can imagine that each attack lasted over an hour, and during that time there was continuous cover fire, so it was understandable where all the empty shells came from.

After Bamboo Ridge the fighting was rough on a regular basis. The new Jap division that had landed was cocky and ready to go. We were not too healthy now. I really had sore feet and dysentery too. Every day or two I'd go to the medics for some paregoric, and that would stop the diarrhea for awhile before it started again. We got 10 new replacements, but within two days they were either wounded or dead. With one guy sleeping and the other two watching, you couldn't talk, so you had a lot of time to think. I just couldn't figure out how all those new guys got wounded so fast while during the same two days none of the old guys had gotten hurt. I thought it must be just bad luck.

I asked one of those new guys what they were told to do in combat. He said, "They just told us to do what the old guys do, and we'd be all right." That must be it. The worst thing you can do in combat is set up a pattern, and that's exactly what they were doing. If one guy went through an area fast for some cover a Jap might not have his rifle up, but if another guy followed he'd be the one to get it. No wonder they were getting shot. Staying on the heels of the old guys was not a healthy thing to do.

I was first scout now. Sometimes it was for the whole platoon and sometimes it was just for a squad or two. I would be as much as 100 yards ahead of the rest and the second scout, Saki Joe, would be 50 yards or so behind me. At other times if it was really bad, the second scout and I would move together. When we stopped for a rest we would put two men out 50 yards on all four sides of the platoon to watch. Having a bunch of guys together in a group made everyone more comfortable and less watchful. That was dangerous. The Japs would stop with no men watching and sometimes I could walk right up on 8 or 10 of them and they didn't see me until I started shooting. Sometimes I could even signal the rest of the guys to join me in surprising them.

The previous first scout had been killed by a knee mortar shell as he was peeking around a tree. I learned that was not a wise thing to do cause if they can see the tree they've got something to aim at even if they don't see you.

As first scout I developed the ability to sense where and how the Japs would be hiding. A lot of times I could walk right up on them and shoot them twice in their holes before they got their gun up. They would sit in their hole with their rifle between their legs maybe sleeping or thinking of home. That would happen more times than you would think it should. I was good at it, and never did lead the boys into an ambush, but I knew more than once the Japs were looking at me through their rifle sights. I often wondered how I looked in their sights.

We went from one hill to the next and really didn't know what we would run into. Usually they'd send a squad or platoon up first to confirm whether or not the Japs were there. Hell, I knew the Japs were up there, they always were. I couldn't see any reason to go up there with a small group just to make contact and fight your way back. That wasn't as easy as they thought. F Company found that out. They had a platoon walk into an ambush on a hill next to us and they were all killed. We could hear it, but couldn't help. Those that weren't killed the Japs put the bayonet to and then ran away.

On one hill we got the mortar boys to blast the Jap positions until a certain time and then to keep shelling but aim long. The Japs thought the mortar attack was still on, so we'd rush up and catch them in their holes while the mortar shells went over our heads. That worked pretty good. Most of the time the Japs would try to haul off their dead and wounded, so you didn't know how successful you were. On this one hill, we found a live one that had been wounded in the head. He laid there brushing the flies away from his wound. A general came up to the top and somebody asked him what we should do with the wounded Jap. His reply was, "Shoot the son of a bitch," so one of the boys shot him. If we'd sent him back to an aid station, I don't know for sure whether he'd have survived or not, but he sure didn't that way.

The Japs left a brand-new machine gun up there too, so we just aimed in their direction and fired the gun until the parts heated and jammed. This was the hill that the 32nd had lost about two weeks before. Their foxholes were still there, and in one was a dead American. He was from Mississippi, and I sent one of his dog tags back. Before that he had just been listed as missing.

Well we started to dig in to hold the hill because it looked like the Japs wanted to fight. We had a machine gun knocked out right after we got the hill. It took a round through the cooling chamber. The 3rd assistant leader got hit and they sent him back to the hospital. The Japs were trying to push us off before we got organized and dug in, but we finally got our positions set and secure and held the hill.

From our positions on this hill we could see some Japs moving in and out of a grass hut that was on kind of a bare hillside on the other side of a big gully. I set my M-1 sights at 1200 yards and started taking shots at them. A mortar guy was beside me and with a pair of field glasses he could track my tracers and see where they were hitting. I had to aim about the thickness of the sight in front of them so the bullet and they got there at the same time. I was the only guy shooting, and I'd get one about every third shot. There wasn't much cover around the hut so they would run back in the hut, and then a guy with the BAR would fire some shells into the hut and they would run back out. We kept that up until I had gotten all of them. That sure was the best way to fight. We were at a nice long distance away, plus they didn't know where we were and weren't firin' back. That was kind of exciting anyway, and sure made our day.

The next morning my platoon was sent up another hill to see if there were any Japs there. We were almost at the top when a shot rang out and I heard an "Oh, Oh!" Right after that a machine gun opened up on us and more rifle shots. I flew into a low spot and another guy hit right beside me, and his BAR started firing by itself. It was pointed towards the Japs so that was good, and after about fifteen shots he got it shut off.

Our lieutenant started to run over to help the wounded man. A machine gun opened up and the lieutenant went head over heels to the ground. I thought they had gotten him, but he had tripped on some barbed wire and was OK. The wire probably saved his life. The boy was wounded in the knee and we didn't dare try to carry him out because the Jap machine was sawing off the grass over our heads. We told him to crawl back part way off the hill and we'd cover him. I knew he was hurting, but he didn't say anything and started crawling back. We couldn't see anything, but laid cover fire over the grass area in front of us to keep the Japs down. That worked just fine cause we got him off and no one else was hurt. He went to the hospital and we never did see him again.

Hill after hill, river after river and our feet kept getting sorer. There were no clean or dry socks and our feet were always wet. They would keep promising us that soon we'd be replaced, but it didn't happen. They said they were short-handed. Our food supply was short also. Occasionally we'd get 10 in one rations. That was the best that the army had given us. They were supposed to feed 10 men for a day. If you had less men you got more food. To supplement our lack of food we traded with the Filipinos for eggs and things. Also we ate lots of coconuts. They were everywhere. The green ones you could puncture and drink the water inside, and once they were ripe you could break them and eat the white meat.

It was so hot, and we sweat so much it was hard to get enough water to drink. We were too far forward for them to bring water to us, so most of the time we put our ponchos up at night to catch the rain water, and fill our canteens next morning. There was water every place, but it wasn't clean. The captain told us never to take drinking water from the river, but then one day we saw him fill his canteen there. When we did fill our canteens from streams, we put some pills in to make it safer, but you never could tell how clean it was. There could be a dead Jap or more upstream from where you were getting your water.

Because the bridges were out, about the only thing that had any luck getting to us was what they called a weasel. It was made by Studebaker and was small and couldn't haul very much, but it did bring ammunition in and haul the wounded and dead out.

One day we had it pretty bad and there was only room to haul the wounded back. Several dead Americans were left until the next day. I didn't see it, but my second scout did, and told me that when they got back up there the next morning chunks of meat had been cut off of the hind ends of our soldiers. There were cooking pots around the area too. He said it sure looked like the Japs had been cooking and eating parts of our boys. Somebody had told us before that they had found instructions in captured Jap manuals that told them how to do that if they couldn't get food. Headquarters was informed and they came up and took a bunch of pictures, but we didn't hear any more about it.

While we were walking down a road a Jap airplane came over us with a bomb on. Most of the time they didn't bomb a few men, usually they were after trucks. This guy probably didn't have a good target and wanted to get rid of the bomb and leave, so we were a handy target. When we saw him rolling in we headed for the ditch. They always said that if you could see the nose of the bomb after it was dropped, you should get down on your knees and pray because you weren't gonna be here long. Well this guy rolled into a dive and dropped the bomb kinda high, and I could see the sides of the bomb so I wasn't too scared. Well, I was still scared though, and kept my head down until she hit and blew. Nobody got hurt and I gave him 20 shots from my BAR.

We were pretty worn out now, but orders came down that we were to go as fast as possible to reach Ormoc Harbor. That was the only good port the Japs had left to unload ships, and if we cut them off from it, we might shorten the fighting with them.

Late in the afternoon we arrived at the port and found that the Japs had all left. You should have seen all the new equipment there. It looked like they had just unloaded ships, because truckloads of new parts, guns, ammunition and even new trucks were all exposed. Usually they would have had it all buried or hidden someplace. For some reason they were all scared off. There weren't many of us to guard the harbor so we dug in between the road and the beach. Our trucks couldn't bring supplies to us anymore because so many bridges were out. They had been using the alligator landing boats to bring stuff into us along the shore. We set up a big gun for our defense, a 57 or 37mm, I can't remember for sure. Our tanks couldn't make it in so no help from them.

That night three Jap ships came in to unload. They didn't realize that we held the harbor and when we started shooting at them they thought it was their own men doing it, and started blinking their signal lights like mad to stop the firing. We were shooting like hell and got one ship on fire. The Japs jumped off the burning ship into the water and were shot before they could reach shore. The ship was in such shallow water it wouldn't sink. The other two ships left and pulled up farther down shore on the other side of the harbor.

The next day we sent a patrol out to investigate where the other two ships had landed. The ships were gone, but before they left they had unloaded ten new Jap tanks. We went down later and shot them all up. The ship up in the harbor burned for two days. We sent some guys out to check it out and there was still one Jap alive on it. I would have thought it would have been too hot for anyone to have survived.

We tried to bury some of the Jap supplies. There was too much to guard, and there was the chance the Japs might slip down during the night and get some of it. Later the engineers came in and buried the ammunition as it wasn't safe to burn.

Our outfit set up a base camp in town next to the harbor. There had been a sugar cane plant there with a narrow gauge rail track that went up into the hills to haul the sugar cane down. The Japs had left the town when we arrived and headed for the hills. Up the rail track a little we found brand new guns that the Japs hadn't had time to set up. One 37mm was still packed in cosmoline to preserve it.

Every day we'd go out on patrol in the hills and look for Japs. At night we'd return to our base camp in town. The medics had set up shop in the cane mill, and I'd go down every day to soak my feet. I had athlete's foot as did most of the boys. Not having clean socks or dry feet was the cause. The soaking didn't help much as we'd be right back out walking on patrol the same day, so our feet stayed sore.

This one day we moved on up the track with a small patrol and I saw a Jap cross the track behind us. I swung around and shot him. We moved into the edge of a cane field and just inside was a path. Now this sugar cane was pretty high, just like a cornfield back home. The path was far enough into the field that the Japs could run up and down it and not be spotted from the rail tracks. Just my sergeant and I were on the path and the rest of the platoon was behind us. It was raining at the time, but the hobnailed boot prints I saw on the path were so fresh there wasn't any water in them. Without speaking, I pointed the tracks out to the sergeant who was fifteen feet to my right. As I looked up I saw a Jap right behind him, so I raised up and shot him. A couple of minutes later he shot one that came out behind me. We weren't sure what to do, but it looked like they were trying to cut us off and ambush us. They knew we were coming and were waiting for us. They liked to do that. F Company got all shot up that way. We stood there thinking and I looked outside the field and saw some bushes and tall grass. The grass was moving even though the wind wasn't blowing. I pointed towards the bushes. We got out a bunch of hand grenades, about six, and threw them over into the bushes. After they went off you ought to have heard the moaning and groaning coming from the brush. I didn't see the Japs, but you sure could hear them. We rounded up the rest of the guys and got the hell out of there as there weren't very many of us. That day we were lucky, nobody got hurt. You had to be careful not to get cut off from your outfit, cause if you did nobody could help you.

They finally brought a few of our tanks in through the harbor to support us. To counter the tanks, the Japs would cover somebody up in the ditch and wait for a tank to come by. When one did they would jump out and put 10 pounds of TNT under it and knock the tank out and blow themselves up too. I saw one tank get blown up that way, killing two boys inside. After that we'd have a couple guys walk along with the tank and kill the Japs when they jumped out.

Most of the time the tanks had a rough time going anyplace, because the roads were so muddy. When they could, they would go in pairs. One tank would cover one side of the road and the second one would get the other. When we came up on a village the tanks would fire their machine guns into a few of the huts, and the Japs thinking they had been spotted, would run. We'd get them then, and put an end to their troubles. Sometimes the tanks would just fire into the bamboo along the road, and that would get them running too.

Some nights we'd go out on a patrol and stay out overnight. One night it rained so much that the next morning there was six inches of water over our hole, and we sat in it most of the night. There was no water in sight when we dug the hole. I guess you could call that a GI bath.

Finally we got some more troops, and instead of moving from the town out to the foothills on patrol each day, we just set up camp in the fields. We had to cut the cane down with a machete for a hundred yards around our foxholes. That was hard work, but if we hadn't done that the Japs could have gotten close enough to lob grenades in our holes. It seemed like a lot of the nights it rained, which made it miserable in our foxholes. The Japs were dug in only 150 yards or so from us, and when they would stick their heads up we'd shoot at them, and when our heads were up they would shoot at us.

Sitting in that hole one night I got to thinking, "My God, that fellow sitting out there, I don't even know that Jap, but if he puts his head up I'm gonna shoot him. I've never met or seen him, so how could I be mad enough to shoot him? And how could he be mad at me, who he's never met, but would shoot me if he had the chance. He must have a better place to be, a home and a mother. I know I have. What the devil am I doing halfway around the world in a sugar cane field trying to kill someone I've never met? I couldn't possibly be mad at him, cause I've never met him. I guess that's how war is."

The next morning we went out on patrol and found a wounded Jap. I don't know how he got out there, maybe they carried him there for us to take care of. He could speak pretty good English and said he'd only been in the army a couple of months. That proved that they must be getting hard up for men if after only two months they had him on some island fighting. He was an older man too. He told what island he came from, and we carried him down to our medics. Their response was, "What are you carrying that dirty Jap down here for? We have enough of our own men to care for. Why don't you shoot him? Don't bring any more of them in." I guess they took care of him, at least it looked as if they were planning to. They used to tell us to bring Japs in so they could get information from them, so it was hard to know what to do.

One prisoner we got was pretending to be a Filipino. He was trying to sell or trade eggs like the Filipinos do, but we found out he was a Jap. In fact we found out he was on Bamboo Ridge when we attacked. He told us how many men were killed and how they dragged their dead back. Most of the time you couldn't get prisoners though, cause they just wouldn't give up.

On the day before Christmas we were out on patrol and killed 27 Japs and not one of our boys got hurt. The first four we got out of a little hut on the edge of a village. Saki Joe and I went up to the hut while the rest of the squad covered us. When we got up there four Japs ran out the back and we dropped all four. One kinda fell on his gun and when we approached him he tried to get his gun out. It looked like he had been shot through the buttocks and the bullet had come out his stomach. Joe had three shells left in his clip and fired them into the guy's back. That didn't kill him, for he was still trying to get the gun up when the sergeant walked up and shot him in the head. I took a knife and opened up their shirts and pants looking for souvenirs. A lot of the time they had coins sewn inside of their clothes for good luck, but all the ones I found had bad luck.

Some Filipinos had been following us around that day waiting for us to clean out their village. They were scared, but liked to have you think they were brave. When we had the Japs all searched the Filipinos crowded around, and one little devil grabbed the hair around this dead Jap's privates and pulled it, kicked him, cussed him, and kicked him some more. I said to myself, "Boy if that Jap was alive, you'd be running in the other direction." I had given the Jap guns to Saki Joe to hold and some Filipinos came up and wanted them. They said they were guerillas and had killed many Japs. I told Saki to give me one of the rifles and I bent the barrel around a coconut tree and gave it to the Filipino. You should have seen the look on his face. I guess he thought I had been here too long and so did I. Saki Joe said, "Why did you do that?" I said, "The less guns in the hills the better. They are scared anyway, so with that bent barrel they can shoot around corners of houses." They didn't get any of the guns, we just didn't trust them. Sometimes the Japs would be carrying our M-1s and ammunition. These guns we didn't destroy. We wanted to be the only ones with guns. That's the best way to fight a war. We figured the Filipinos might get on whichever side they thought was winning at the time.

At another village that day we came upon a path that had six huts along it. The sergeant was with me and he was going to provide cover for me with his tommy gun while I checked out the first hut. There wasn't any glass in the window so I just poked my rifle in and almost shot this Filipino lying on a bench. My safety was off and I had a lot of pressure on the trigger. Without warning a Filipino woman walked through the doorway and I almost shot her too. She kept saying, "Good morning, good morning." I asked if there were any Japs around and she said good morning again and indicated the next hut, 50 yards or so away. I told my sarge that she said there were Japs in the next hut and about that time 9 Japs came out the back of the hut with packs on. Well the sergeant raised his old tommy gun up to shoot and lo and behold it just went "click". Here he was gonna protect me with a dumb gun that wouldn't even fire. What a deal. I shot the last one in line and the others dropped their packs and really started running. The rest of the squad was behind us and could see them so they opened up. I just kept shooting at them and the sergeant got his gun working, so we got the last 8. Four more ran out of another hut and one didn't have a shirt on. The first time I shot at him I knew I hit him cause he went down, but he was back up and the second shot put him down again. By golly if he didn't get up and it took the third shot before he stayed down. I couldn't believe a man could take that much, it was amazing.

At another shack one of the guys spotted a Jap inside and fired right through the shack and almost got me when the bullets came out the other side. We didn't do that anymore. I guess you learn as you fight, and if you live, you're lucky. We all got on one side of a shack after that, or we didn't take it at all.

On Christmas day we were supposed to be able to rest, but some dummy went out and found four more Japs so we had to send a patrol out to get them. I heard later that a lot of the Japs in the hills around there were the engineers and supply people from the beach and that's why they weren't very good fighters. A lot of the time they would just drop their guns and run. One day a bunch walked right in where we were eating dinner and we hollered at them to give up, but they just took off running and we had to shoot them all.

On that Christmas Day my present was a fruitcake in a tin. There were ants inside, but it looked so good that we put it in the fire and the ants that didn't leave got eaten. My hard candy wasn't any good as it was like glue and my cheese had worms in it. We did find some Jap candy and that was good. I was going to try some of their canned fish but they didn't look too appetizing with the heads on.

December 25, 1944

"I shot a Jap all by myself yesterday, which was the first here. I helped shoot another one or two also."

"I received the cake you sent last night, and was it ever good. I got the box Moons sent too. I heard from Mrs.

Rowley that Dad got a deer. I have two Jap pens and one pencil set."

"I might not weigh so much now as we have been having hell lately. I hope this is over pretty soon. I hope your Christmas is better than what we have over here."

December 28, 1944

"Boy, that cake you sent was really good. We had walked about ten miles that day and had C rations for dinner. It was OK yet when it got here."

"Does Harvey have to go to the army in January? I sure hope not."

"It doesn't seem like it could be cold back home because it is hotter here than what it ever was at home. I hope I am not here when summer comes."

"I will close now and send some Jap money home."

It seemed like we would clean the Japs out of one area and the next day we'd have to go back to the same area and do it all over again. We couldn't figure out what they were doing. We thought that maybe they were just trying to get back to the beach and get some of their supplies. We very seldom took any prisoners, they just never gave up. I did hear that F Company found a Jap hospital and there were about 20 Japs lying around inside with various wounds. This one guy from the company was so mad about the platoon that got wiped out, he took a BAR and ran it up one side of the beds and back down the other. They were trying to get away but he wiped everybody out. I didn't see it but I heard that's what happened.

The Japs did the same thing though. If they found a wounded American they would just bayonet him, they didn't fool around. That's what I didn't like about the Japs. They were too much with that bayonet. That really scared me. I think I'd have rather been shot, cause I think when they pull that bayonet out it would really hurt.

We sure shot a lot of Japs on our patrols, and it seemed like an awful waste of human lives. You'd have thought they would have come down and just surrendered, cause they just couldn't win. They had nothing to gain anymore.

Sometimes we went quite a ways out on our patrols. On one

instance we came upon this big gully and rather than have everybody exposed, myself being first scout and Saki Joe went down through the gully and up on the other side. There were so many Japs on the other side I couldn't believe it. I fired my gun about 46 times and it got so hot it wouldn't fire anymore, and that really scared me. There still were all kinds of Japs running around, not fighting, just running. The rest of the outfit came over, but by that time the Japs had about disappeared. I had to get another gun after that. The barrel on that one got so hot it burned the wood next to the barrel. They saved guns when somebody was killed or wounded so I didn't have any trouble picking up another.

Sometimes if we weren't going too far I carried a BAR and an M-1. This one morning after crossing a gully we started up a ridge and were walking through this shoulder-high elephant grass. I was the farthest man to the left and the rest were five yards apart to the right. I was really watching my left because I knew if there was to be an ambush from that side I would be the first to get it. An older soldier we called Pop was on my right and he said, "Hold it Heppe." I looked over towards him and just then a Jap popped up out of the grass. I don't know whether he had been hiding or just sleeping and we woke him. I didn't even bring the BAR up, just fired twice from the hip, dropping him. I went over to search him and was about ready to open up his clothes with my knife when he raised up real fast. I had given Pop my gun, plus he had his own and the Jap's, so Pop couldn't shoot. I was getting ready to cut his throat if I had to, but really didn't want to. It didn't take long to realize that with two bullets between the eyes he wasn't going anyplace, and his movement was just a dying impulse. Guess it was just a nervous reaction on my part.

We never searched a Jap unless we saw him killed, because otherwise he might be booby-trapped. On this one I just killed, I found a nice watch in his pocket and a cigarette case. The cigarette case was silver with a Jap flag on one side with the spokes radiating from the red spot. On the other side was just the flag with the red spot. I gave the case to Pop because I didn't smoke. I wished afterwards I'd have kept it cause it would have been worth some money. The watch was nice though, with a compass on it.

The navy was always ready to fork out their cash for about anything we had with Jap markings on it. I could have easily sold the Jap watch for 200 dollars. Rifles would bring 100 dollars, and small packets of Jap money I could get 10 dollars for. Off a dead Jap medic, I got a whole pack of wooden dog tags with names burned on them. Those I could get a couple bucks apiece for. Some guys even took our parachute flares and drew Jap markings on them and sold those to the navy.

Not too far out from shore there was that Jap boat burned right down to the waterline. Another guy and I were kinda looking at it as we walked along. It wasn't real big, maybe 30 feet long. There was a sand bar there that we were walking on and on the other side of the sand bar there was a little pond. As we were looking and walking a big shell hit between us and the burned hulk. We decided that was no place for us. There was no cover in sight except sand, so we took off running back where we had come from. Boy, the next shell hit right where we had been standing, but by that time we were 25 yards away. We didn't stop there either, which was good, because the next shell was not far behind the last one. Finally we reached a sand bank for cover and relaxed. The guy that was with me was a lot older than I, but he actually beat me to the sand bank. We laughed about that. I said, "Boy, you can really run when you get scared." "Yeah," he said, "there wasn't nothin' holding my feet down." We never did see the gun or know where it shot from. The Japs probably had it way up in the hills where they could see the beach, and shot at anything that came around. Later we had to take our outfit through the same area. We did it two or three at a time right through gunfire, but nobody got hurt. Again we were lucky.

On the First of January, 1945, they put our whole company together for a big operation. Apparently a bunch of the Japs were getting formed together for some organized resistance, and we were going out in some new territory for four days to take care of them. Because we weren't coming back for awhile we all had to carry extra machine gun shells.

Things went pretty well the first day. There were lots of Japs in the hills and we managed to kill most of them we ran into. We moved around one Jap foxhole that was out in a clear field. It wasn't worth trying to get him cause some of our guys might get killed. We had the battle won and didn't want any more of our men killed if we could help it. Those Japs we went around or missed would eventually try to make it back to their line and we'd get them then. That was the way the game was played. We would try to get them to give up, but they only ran and we would have to shoot them, which was bad.

That night they tried to get us. We were in our holes and the Japs would shoot in our direction trying to get us to return fire and give away our positions. We were smarter now, and didn't do that. Besides, you couldn't see to hit them anyway. You never knew which direction they would come from. Those that we had passed up during the day would be trying to make it back and run into our lines. At night, most of the Japs we killed with grenades. If we had enough grenades, we might have as many as fifty by each hole. They worked good and didn't give away our position.

My hole was up on kind of a high bank. It's a good thing too, cause a Jap threw a charge up close to the hole, but it just rolled back down and went off below. They weren't far out in front of us through the night. I could hear one rackin' a shell in his rifle chamber, and another one digging his hole. Your nerves ran high when you could hear them close, but couldn't see them.

The next morning just before it got daylight, I could see a whole bunch of Japs on another hillside. It was a long ways away, but I opened up on them and they ran up the hill. I don't know whether I hit any of them, but I sure made them move.

There were two dead Japs not too far from my hole that had been there for a few days and were really starting to stink. You could see flies crawling over their faces, in and out of their noses and mouths. Eating my lunch, I just knew where those flies buzzing around me had been, and it wasn't appetizing.

Sometimes you'd be out on patrol and see a couple Japs lying there and you didn't know for sure whether they were dead or playing possum with you. At times if they had been there for a couple of weeks, there would just be skeletons left inside the uniforms, and skulls looking at you from inside the helmets. It was so hot that everything deteriorated fast. Most of the time the Japs would hide their dead by burying them in a foxhole. The trouble was that sometimes the bodies would be stiff and they couldn't get the body bent to go down in the hole. In that case they would just shove them down head first and mound up the dirt to cover the feet sticking out of the ground. That worked until the first big rain came and washed the mounded dirt away and then there would be two feet sticking out of the ground. One time in some tall grass I tripped on a pair of feet sticking out. They never did make an effort to mark the graves. Another time I tripped over a guy's shoe with the leg still in it up to the knee. I don't know where the rest of him was. It must have been shot right off.

They set up a 4.1 mortar on the road to support this company operation we had going, so we called in for some rounds for a bunch of Japs in a bamboo thicket ahead. We were waiting for the shells to hit in the thicket when one hit behind us. That really scared us and we hit the dirt until they got their aim adjusted to the thicket. We were really lucky no one got hurt. Starting up towards the thicket a machine gun opened up on us and boy did I ever jump for cover. By the time we could see the smoke come out of the grass he had left. All we would find was some empty shells. He did it again, but if he didn't hit someone on the first shot we were under cover. You were always scared he might get lucky sometime. We would get a few now and then, but most were just trying to get away from us. If they would have given up it would have been a lot better for both of us, and a lot more men would live. They just couldn't ever win the battle here now.

It was on the Fourth of January and our platoon had been moving through some tall grass when one of our boys was shot in the leg. I stayed there with him waiting for the medics to arrive and carry him out. The grass was so tall they might miss him if someone didn't stay. I was down on my knees with my rifle propped up in front of me, when all of a sudden something went off in my face which knocked me right on my can. I couldn't figure out what had happened to me. Perhaps my own rifle had accidentally gone off and I had shot myself. My neck hurt and burned terribly as I crawled back to my sergeant who was just behind me. We both looked at my rifle and there was a bullet hole right by the bayonet lug on the barrel. My neck had been hit by ricochetting splinters from the gun and the Jap bullet. The Jap had been so close when he fired that there were powder burns all over my neck.

When the medics came after the guy shot in the leg, I was so much worse off, bleeding a lot, they took me instead. A couple hundred yards back at the aid station they gave me two bottles of blood plasma. The doctor held a bandage on my neck so tight I could hardly breathe. I didn't know whether the fragments had put a hole in my jugular vein or not, but the doctor told me later he didn't think I was gonna make it. I told him I figured I was going to make it all the time.

They finally got the bleeding stopped and they put me back on the stretcher and we headed for the road that was a half mile away. Those four guys carrying the stretcher did a beautiful job. We went up and down gullies and some real rough terrain which would have been difficult for just a single man to walk. You couldn't have asked for a smoother ride. When we reached the road it was obvious that it had been a bad day. All our stretchers were taken up with the wounded, none left to carry out the dead yet. They put me on a jeep and we headed towards the Jap airfield we had captured earlier. They had given me some morphine, so a lot I don't remember. Morphine kinda half knocks you out. Time seems to go real fast, a hour seems like minutes. I do remember that when we arrived at the airport that the place now looked like a junkyard. Wrecked airplanes were stacked on both sides of the runway. Some were those that the Japs had blown up, and other had crash-landed after returning all shot up from their missions. I couldn't believe how many there were. They put me on a plane and I was on my way to a hospital in New Guinea.

In New Guinea they took three pieces of shrapnel out of my neck and told me how lucky I was to have made it.

The Jap magazine I found showed the victorious Japanese when they first took the Philippines. Their commanders were all happy with their success. There were lots of pictures of captured Americans and their equipment. I bet now they would have a little trouble looking so happy.

New Guinea

MRS ELIZABETH HEPPE
 =RT ONE ORLEANS MICH=
 =REGRET TO INFORM YOU YOUR SON PRIVATE
FIRST CLASS VERNON W. HEPPE WAS SLIGHTLY
WOUNDED IN ACTION FOUR JANUARY ON LEYTE
YOU WILL BE ADVISED AS REPORTS OF CONDITION
ARE RECEIVED=
 J A VLIO THE ADJUTANT GENERAL
January 1945

"Well it is me again and I guess by this time you have heard the bad news. I am on a hospital ship and I am OK. You need not worry. I was hit in the right side of my neck by some shrapnel. I was really lucky for I had the rifle in front of my face and the bullet hit my rifle and broke some shrapnel off it and that is what hit me. That is what I call luck."

"New Year's Day I killed a Jap from about 10 feet and I have a nice wristwatch from him. It runs too fast but it looks good. I will send it home the first chance I get."

"I don't want you to worry about me as I am eating fine. I am a little poor so I can use it."
January 16, 1945

"I am OK now. I still might have a little shrapnel in my neck yet, but it doesn't hurt me."

"Well brother, how many muskrats did you get this year?"

"I haven't received all of my Christmas presents yet. I only got three of them. The cake from Mother, a box from Moons, and a box from Elrena."

"How much snow have you got? Boy, is it hot here on this ship. I would like to see some of that snow again. Bet I could wash your face in it, and Robert's too, at the same time."

In New Guinea they took three pieces of shrapnel out of my neck and told me how lucky I was to have made it. Yes, I was lucky to be OK, but I wasn't lucky to be in New Guinea. To begin with, what you weren't wearing in the hospital was sure to disappear. I had a Jap flag and a lot of wooden dog tags. They all came up missing along with other personal things.

January 23, 1945

"I will drop you a couple of lines to let you know how I am getting along. I am at a base hospital in Dutch New Guinea, and it is about the same as anywhere you go down here. Hot and lots of rain."

"I am pretty good now, and you couldn't tell I was ever hurt except for some powder burns on my neck and some small shrapnel. I can say that I am one of the luckiest boys in the army. If it hadn't hit my rifle I wouldn't be here now, and you can see how close he was by the powder burns."

"I am in the 54th General Hospital and have found some of the boys from our company who were wounded before I was. Some of the bad ones went back to the U.S.A."

"My nerves are shot too, I guess, for it is hard for me to sit down and write a letter. I just want to be on the go all the time and it seems hard to remember anymore. Just can't seem to be able to think good yet, but 90 days on the front is a long time. I can't remember all the boy's names in our company. My hands even shake a little. I will get a rest here, and I don't know when, but I think that I will go back to the old company."

"Boy, would it ever be swell to get to come home now for 30 days. I wouldn't want to ever go back to camp again I guess. I have 19 months over now, so maybe when I get those 24 in I might get sent back, and get a furlough. Hope so anyway."

"I could get $100 for my Jap watch, but I want to keep it

because I really killed the Jap who had it on. One boy said he would give me $200 when he was paid, but you know how that is."

January 25, 1945

"I had three teeth filled today and that wasn't any fun. They should be OK now for another six months. Seems like since I came in the army my teeth have been getting worse."

"We have shows here three times a week, and they sure seem nice again. The Red Cross has a building here, but they have a hard time getting things too. I sure would like to get behind 10 gallons of ice cream and go to town on it. They have a PX here, but it sells out in about one hour after they open. They don't have much in the first place."

"There are army nurses here at the hospital and lots of soldiers. There is a camp of WACs over here too, but I haven't seen any around yet."

"I would like some of that noncombat duty myself for a change. I am going to try for it when I get back or maybe even before I leave here. The more battles you have the worse it is on you. You hate the second one a lot more than the first one and the third one will be almost too much. A lot of them couldn't take it on Leyte, and we were up on the front so long which was very bad too. When I left there weren't half as many men in our company as when we landed."

January 31, 1945

"I am kind of mad this morning. You see someone took my Jap flag and pen set last night. Also a couple more things which I wanted to keep, so you can see why I am mad. In all it would have been worth over $100. I still have my watch yet. I had it in my shirt pocket. Next time I will know better I guess. I will sell everything and let someone else worry about losing it."

"I might be out of the hospital in a couple days now."

"I haven't received any mail yet. About the time I go back my mail will start coming here."

"One of the boys from our company left yesterday.

There are a lot of them going back to the U.S., but they are hurt bad."

From the hospital I was sent to a replacement camp which was way overcrowded. We were living in tents and doing work details for entertainment. For a long time I didn't even have a rifle. To not have a rifle was kinda like walkin' around without your pants. There were still some do or die Japs up in the hills too, and occasionally they would fire a few rounds down in the camp and everybody would head for a ditch. Most of the time the Japs were just interested in getting something to eat though. They had guards on each end of the mess hall, but one night a Jap got inside and when the guards tried to get him one guard shot the other, while the Jap got away.

The Japs weren't the only reason they were guarding the mess hall. They were feeding 3000 men out of one mess hall, and there just never seemed to be enough food. The food wasn't good either. Unfortunately we were located too close to Australia, so we had a steady diet of old sheep. We had so much mutton stew that to this day I can hardly look a sheep in the face.

We were placed on work details to unload the mutton off the ships and the way it was handled never looked too clean either. The sheep carcass was cut in half and put in a cheesecloth bag. We'd be walking right on top of it as we loaded it from the refrigerated compartments into the nets that were lowered to the trucks waiting outside. The trucks weren't even that clean. They had probably hauled garbage that morning. Ground beef also arrived in banded 50 pound boxes, but we never got any of that. Probably that went to the hospital and officers mess. Every time we showed up at the officers mess with a load of mutton, they would just tell us to let the rest of the army have it. They were getting better food somehow.

Working on KP proved to be a good deal because you could usually manage to slip out with some oranges, apples or maybe even a chunk of ground beef. In that case we'd get a little fire going out back and fry that up for ourselves.

I had my own ways to supplement the short food supply. They would have a bunch of cooks detailed to get food ready for the next day, and when they showed up for work late at night I'd slip right in with them. We all wore the same type of uniform and they didn't recognize that I wasn't a cook. I'd only have to work for a couple of hours and I'd get extra to eat.

February 5, 1945

"I am out of the hospital now and waiting to go back to my old company. I am at a casual camp now. The eats are not very good here."

"Well, I was paid up until Jan. 31st this year, so I have some money which I would like to send home. Money isn't any good here, as you can't buy anything."

"It is hotter here than any place I have been yet, and that is saying a lot."

"I was on detail yesterday and the day before. They seem to have lots of them here. They have WACs (womens army corps) here and one day I was working right beside them. They work in the motor pool painting trucks. I was driving a truck myself that day and it wouldn't be a bad job if I could do it every day. Better than going back to the front lines."

"I got new clothes here a couple days ago, and an old beat-up rifle which isn't any good."

February 7, 1945

"Dad, it has been a long time since I wrote you a letter. I will put a money order for $100 in this one which you can put in the bank for me. I have another $65 which I will send in my next letter."

"Well I was just reading the news tonight and the war sounds pretty good to me. Maybe one more year and it will be over."

"We moved yesterday and we have a lot better place now. It is cleaner and a lot better mess hall, but the food is the same."

"Do you need an extra man this spring? I know one who would like to help. Ha, Ha."

February 9, 1945

"I went to a show last night at the hospital, and it wasn't bad. It was a stage show and I think it was put on by the USO. I went back and saw some of the boys who were in with me.

Most of them are going back to the U.S. and are they ever happy about it, and who wouldn't be? They are in bad shape, so maybe they are not so lucky after all."

"If they keep me over here long enough I might save some money before the war ends. I wish it would end right now so that we could all come home. A lot of the boys down here have 36 and 40 months overseas and I have only 20 so I will be here a long time yet."

February 13, 1945

"Well I am still at the same place yet, and it is about the same except that I am working now. They are trying to make us feel at home by working us I guess, but it isn't my idea of home. I guess it is better to work than sleep so much because the time goes faster."

"How about old Jake this winter? Is he going to make it until I get back? He must be 10 years old this March, isn't he? Boy, he was the best dog I ever had. I bet he wouldn't remember me any more."

"I will have two mail bags full of mail when I get back to my old company. I hope it won't be too long before I get there. I wrote them and said I was coming back and for them to hold my mail."

"Have the boys been cutting wood this winter, and what about Harvey and the army? You better try and keep him out because Dad needs him."

In New Guinea they drove on the opposite side of the road. I couldn't understand why we did that. Even if it was the local way, we were the only ones to have any vehicles to drive and it could become downright dangerous if when you turned a corner you forgot to get back on your side. They didn't use pesos for money either, as they did in the Philippines. Here they used guilders, something else inherited from the Dutch.

We called the natives Fuzzy Wuzzies. They were small people that didn't wear many clothes, and moved around together in families of 10 to 12. The Japs couldn't get along with them and we were told not to mess with them either. They had blowguns with poison darts and didn't seem afraid of us. The army had built a new road and you would see their little groups along it watching what we were up to. The people were really homely looking with bones in their noses. The women had long tits that looked like bananas. They had a cord tied around them, I guess to keep them from bouncing up and putting an eye out when they ran.

I worked in supply one day and finally got myself some new socks. Shortly after that they issued us some new clothes to wear. I got an extra shirt by going down without one and wearing one back. I even got a sweater, which worked good at night in the Philippines. It was too thick for the mosquitoes to bite through. I got a new rifle cleaning rod and a rifle that was junk. It didn't even have any rifling left in the barrel. I couldn't believe they would issue me a gun like that. Another fellow in my tent had a good one, and he wasn't going back to his outfit as a rifleman, so we traded guns.

Being in New Guinea was really a waste of time. Lots of work details and no entertainment available. No movies, no ball playing and bad food. Even the mail hadn't caught up to us. We were all ready to go back to our units, but I guess it just took time to make the ships available to take us.

When I finally did get on a ship and reunited with my outfit in Leyte, they were real surprised to see me. The aid station that took me in hadn't known my name, and they told my outfit that a guy that came in with a neck wound had died. They had mistaken me with a guy from E Company that had died of a neck wound. I guess that's why my mail wasn't forwarded.

Reunion On Leyte

It was good to be back with my old company. While I was away new replacements had arrived and were being trained. Our tents were set up in a big sandy area and they even had them all in a row, and were having inspections again. Things were certainly better than what we had in combat, but not completely modern. At the end of our row of tents they had a pipe in the ground about two feet high that you peed in. Then, not too far away from that was a 25 foot trench for the rest of the business. You just straddled the trench and let her go. The paper you had to bring with you, but they kept a shovel handy to cover it up afterwards. The trench wasn't too bad if only two were using it, cause you could be on opposite ends facing away from the other. Things were less private if three had to use it at the same time.

The shower was just a big tank on four posts with a pipe down over your head. You could have all the hot water you wanted. Ha, Ha.

Our tent was right next to the road and we always had the sides up for air. Quite often the Filipino girls would walk past and this one guy in my tent would lay there naked when they came past. He would have his oversized penis in his hand and wave it at them saying, "Pow, Pow for five pesos." They all would talk at the same time and wave their hands. They sounded like a bunch of turkeys. Never did they take his five pesos, but they still kept coming around fairly often.

This was supposed to be a rest camp, but they still made you go out and work, unloading ships and stuff. Most of the time unloading ships wasn't a good deal, but one time it did prove to be rewarding. This big ship came in that had been shot up by the Japs, and we were detailed to help unload her. She was loaded full of PX supplies, things we hadn't seen in a long time. On the ship we helped unload beer, cigarettes and lots of other goodies into the big cargo nets that were lowered over the side into trucks. We finally got smart and had one of our trucks get in line with the others. When it was filled, we hustled it back to camp and hid all the stuff by our tents.

We had a good variety of things, cans of cherries, fruit cocktail, sugar, and cigarettes. A lot of it we buried right underneath our tents. Later one of the guys opened a big carton of cigarettes, and got caught by a couple of MPs snooping around. The captain came by to see what was happening and the MPs explained why they had arrested the guy. The captain said, "You release this man in my custody, I'll take care of him." Those MPs were privates, and MPs are not known to be too smart anyway, so they released him to the captain. When they were gone the captain said, "I don't care what you guys do, you've been through a lot. Just don't get caught at it next time." We were a little more careful exposing our loot after that.

The engineers and artillery guys had a PX set up down at the beach for their people, but they wouldn't let us buy anything out of it. They issued tickets to their people, which you needed to get in. It didn't seem right. We were the guys up front doing all the fighting and yet we were treated as outcasts. We were able to get things on the Filipino black market with pesos or by trading.

I'm not sure how we got it, but somehow we got ahold of a portable Australian baking oven. The captain put a shift of cooks on at night baking pies for us, and our buried cans of fruit and sugar from the ship provided a steady source of ingredients for the pies. We had all the pie we could eat. If there was any left over the cooks would get after us, "You guys eat up that pie, we're going to make a fresh batch tonight."

The guys in H Company couldn't figure out how we were getting the pies. We told them that their cooks must be sellin' them short. We'd even invite them over occasionally and give them some. Before we got through we had H Company believing their cooks were screwing them and they weren't getting their share.

Around the beach area where we were at, the sea got a little rough. We used to be able to go out swimming, but a couple of guys disappeared so they stopped that. They had some ducks there, like the one I almost drowned in. They said we were gonna take them out in the sea to unload a ship, and I said I wasn't going. I was ordered to get on board even if I didn't want to. Not too far out from shore I jumped out and swam back to the beach. Too many bad memories in that thing for me, I didn't trust them. I waited for two days back at camp by myself, worrying as to whether or not I'd be court-martialed when they returned. Fortunately the sergeant didn't turn me in so nothing came of it.

February 25, 1945

"Well I am back with my old company again and I have been reading my old mail. I nowhere near have it all read yet. I got around 75 letters and there were 34 from Elrena."

"I received my Christmas presents and they were in bad shape. The candy was all soft and ran all over the box, but some of it was good yet. I think there were about nine presents in all. Elrena sent me another box. See, I always said she was a swell girl. It looks to me like I better only buy my ticket to Kansas when I get back to the U.S. Ha, Ha."

"Well, the food isn't so bad now, and that is OK by me. It was swell to get back and see the boys once more."

February 26, 1945

"I will write a letter to the best mother I ever knew or ever hope to know. It is really fun to answer your swell letters."

"I got the money off Japs that we killed on patrol duty. We always look in their pockets if we have time and the Japs aren't shooting at us. I must have looked about 25 or 30 dead ones over myself."

"Boy would I have liked to have had some of your Thanksgiving dinner. Harvey and Robert are lucky to have a mother who can cook like you. For Thanksgiving we had C rations and that old chicken they gave us with no way to cook it."

"Yes, the people here are all Filipinos and they help us more by keeping out of our way than anything else I can think of."

"I bet after Dad got his deer so quick this year he had to get a new hat because the old one wouldn't fit any more. Ha, Ha. It's better when he gets one every year because then he can change stories. Otherwise he would have to tell the same one for two years or until he got another deer. Ha, Ha."

"Mother, there isn't anything I need over here so don't send me any presents unless I ask for them. The mail is so hard to get in here. I know you like to send me stuff, but I am getting along good with what I have."

"Those pictures of the dog are swell."

February 27, 1945

"Harvey, I guess you don't know how lucky you are that you didn't pass for the army. I know you are wishing you had passed, but right now I feel the other way about it, and so does everyone else."

"I have another rifle now and it is almost new."

"The day before I was wounded I had some fun. We had some Japs running about 50 yards away and it was like shooting ducks. I can't tell you how many were killed, but it was a lot of them. I wouldn't want to be in their army, Ha, Ha."

"Say the cows did pretty good this last year from what Mother writes me. Dad didn't have to pay much income tax this year. He is always afraid that it will be so much, but in the end it isn't so bad."

"Say, now that you won't have to go to the army you will have more time with the girls. Mother said it would be nice to have a daughter-in-law so why don't you make her happy? I will even let you have my old bed and live in my room if you want to. Ha, Ha."

February 27, 1945

"I have had two rides on hospital ships now, and they are pretty nice to ride on, but most of the boys can't enjoy them."

"I had a ride on an airplane from the airfield to where the hospital ship was. I didn't mind it at all. I liked it. We took off two times and of course we landed two times too. It was a C-47 plane. The reason I went by plane was the roads were muddy and a long ways around the island."

"I have three combat missions to my credit now and we will get a ribbon for this last one with two stars on it. I will have three stars on my Purple Heart ribbon. I would trade all of them and a lot more to get home again."

"The flag was taken at night with the rest of my things. I had some Jap money, dog tags, billfold, my pocket bible, address book and some of my own money. I had them all in a little red cross bag on my bed. It made me mad as hell, but I couldn't do much about it."

"I heard Snyder was OK."

"We have swell eats now, or they look swell after C rations and 10 in 1 rations. We do have pretty good pie sometimes and lots of it, so tell Harvey he has nothing on me. Boy he is lucky to be able to stay home and eat those fresh eggs, butter, milk and green things from the garden."

"Say those nuts are the best thing to send overseas. Candy gets soft and starts to run out of the box. Send me 5 pounds of nuts sometime and I mean hickory nuts this time. All we have are coconuts and I can hardly look at them anymore."

February 27, 1945

"Mother, I will keep trying to answer your old letters and hope you don't mind too much that I am slow."

"I am glad you got a new coat this year. There isn't anything too good for my mother, and I think the others feel the same way. Say, maybe Harvey can fix you up with that daughter-in-law you would like to have. He has more time to look around than what I do. Don't forget about little Robert either. Ha, Ha."

"I was very sorry to read about Raymond Wagner getting killed. He was only overseas 36 days, which isn't very long. I always wanted to look him up. He was a nice fellow, but I always say when your time is up you have to go and you just can't miss it anyway."

"Those pictures of the boys are swell and Jake looks OK too."

"Yes the girls here would like to marry some soldier and I have heard of a couple cases, but not me. Say Mother, I am glad you like her picture and letters because we both agree that Elrena is OK. Ha, Ha."

March 1, 1945

"I will try and write you a couple lines tonight to try and make up for all of what you and Mother have done for me. I could never see it so when I was home, as I can now. I still can remember you telling me that someday I would say that, and I am not ashamed to say it either. If I spent the rest of my life trying to pay you back I still couldn't do it. I don't know what the future holds for us, but I hope it isn't too dark. I don't think God will let us down now, as he never has before. I can still remember when you let me take your car and I am very glad you did because I have never forgotten it. Since I came in the army and hear other boys talk of home and what my home is, I can see I am much richer in some things than they are and money won't buy them either. Harvey is a swell boy too and he is old enough now to get by. But Robert might not stay on the right road all the time. He is the kind of a guy who wants to look all the roads over and if you do that you are bound to be on the wrong road some of the time. But I guess you and Mother can take care of him."

"I see that the cows did pretty good this last year and you should have made some money. Say, did the corn picker pay for itself this fall? You can make money cutting wood now and I would get it out if I were you while the price is high."

"Now my candle is almost burned out so I have to close for this time, and now will say good night to the best father and mother in the world."

March 3, 1945

"I sent home some pictures of Japs. It is a book which I found down by some little old town the first week or so. It is a book of the battle when the Japs took the island in 1942."

"Well how is everything going back on the farm? Won't be long before the spring rains come and then you will have to start spring work. It doesn't seem to be any different over here in the weather except it rains more in the winter and might be a little hotter in the summer."

"I have read all of the old hometown newspapers, so I

know all the old news anyway."

In March we were making preparations for our next island landing. Considerable time was spent practicing our packing procedures. What went in last were the priority items that should be available when we landed. The mortar shells went on the bottom, and I could see by its priority that extra food would not be available real fast. It never did seem a real priority in the army. On Kwajalein we fought on empty stomachs. In Leyte if it hadn't been for coconuts, bananas and the trades we made for food with the Filipinos, we would have been in bad shape. It rained so much the roads went to pieces and became big mud holes making food scarce. First priority was the wounded, second bringing up more ammunition and the last food.

March 5, 1945

"Boy is it ever hot over here now. Our tent is so hot that you can't stand it very long."

"So you think you could keep me busy on the old farm now? I sure would like to be there and try it. Maybe after the war I can work in the Reed Factory and help at home too, like I did before. It doesn't seem to be what I want for some reason or other. It would be fun to spend six months at home just to cut wood for you for half. Ha, Ha. Anything would be good after this workout."

"Harvey is a lot better off at home than he would be over here and he should be happy. Tell him that I will take care of his end over here if he will take care of my end back there, but that doesn't mean my girl friends. He should be able to do a man's work now, but I could beat him loading hay yet. Ha, Ha."

"So old Jake is really showing his age now. Boy, I would like to see him once more anyway. Can he still hunt yet?"

March 6, 1945

"So Dad is on some farm board now. Maybe he can fix me up when I come home. Ha, Ha. But who wants to be a farmer? Could be that maybe I do, and don't know it yet."

"I have a picture here of Victor's little boy. I told him I couldn't tell who it looked like because I hadn't seen his milkman or iceman. Ha, Ha. He said it looked like him but I almost forgot what he looked like now."

"Boy is it ever hot over here. You could use this heat a lot better than what we can."

March 7, 1945

"Dear Harvey—so it is too cold for you to work in the woods? I can see you don't do much or you wouldn't get cold working. Ha, Ha."

"What is the trouble with the big tractor now? It sure has done a lot of work. It paid for itself two times and then some. Say how much money did you take in this fall picking corn, and what did the corn bring Dad that he sold for seed?"

"Say how does the milking machine run now? You never say a word about it in your letters. I have forgotten how to use it so when I come home you will have to use it. Ha, Ha. I don't even think I could milk a cow with or without the machine."

"Say, I am sending you some Jap money and if you can get anything out of it I want half. I sold some for $3 and $5 each down here."

March 9, 1945

"The last letter you wrote, Katherine was staying home from school with something or other. I couldn't make out in your last letter what it was she had. Maybe you didn't have it spelled right because Webster hadn't ever heard of it either, for it wasn't in the dictionary."

"Mother, you can tell Mildred that I think of her too a lot, and the rest of them too."

"You asked me a lot of questions about coming home and all of that. We don't know as much about what is going on as you do back home. Once you get overseas, it is pretty hard to get back home again."

"Say, I have a bad cold myself now, and in this hot weather it makes it feel worse than what it really is. It seems to be in my head mostly. Now I have to close for this time and get to bed. I need lots of rest the Doc said."

Towards the end of our stay on Leyte we went out in small boats and practiced climbing up the net onto the deck of the big ships. It was hard work and I felt real sick. I didn't get seasick anymore, but my stomach sure was in bad shape. I was told that I would have to tough it out for the day because they couldn't make a trip back just for me and I couldn't go up on the big ship. I leaned over the side and threw up. Some of it ended up on the edge of the ship and in the puddle was a six or seven inch worm that looked like a night crawler. The worm worked his way over the edge I guess cause next time I looked he was gone.

Next our engine quit and had to be worked on. I complained enough that they finally tied me in a basket and the big ship's winch hauled me up to the deck. They took me into the ship's hospital and I told them how I felt and about the worm. The doctor said, "Well did you save it?" "Save it?" I asked. "Yes, there are tons of different kinds of worms so if you don't have it there's nothing we can do for you." Well that was kind of disgusting. They lowered me back down in the basket so I could suffer some more. That was the only worm I threw up. I didn't see any more. I probably picked it up drinking water out of the rivers. You couldn't help it though. When you're in combat you have to have water, so you fill your canteen the best place you can find, put the pills in to treat it, and hope for the best. You also had to be careful and not go barefoot cause there were worms that would burrow in the bottom of your feet and lay eggs too.

We also had to take tablets for Malaria. It didn't cure it, just warded off the symptoms. We probably didn't smell too good either, but everybody was the same so it would have been hard to notice. By mid afternoon our fatigues would be soaked with sweat and they would stay that way until the next morning. When the sun came up we'd start to dry out, but in the afternoon we'd be right back where we started. Our uniforms were all streaked up from the salt we sweat out. We never had clean clothes and only one extra pair of socks. That extra pair we carried in our helmet, but as heavy as those socks were, they couldn't be expected to last forever. Our feet were always wet and always sore from crossing rivers and rice paddies.

There was only one good thing about crossing rice paddies. If the Japs fired mortar at you it would just fall in the mud and go poop.

Unless it hit you directly you didn't get hurt. Otherwise the paddies were a miserable place to be. The mud was knee-deep and really tired you out to walk through it. You had to rest standing up because there was no place to sit except in the mud.

One thing I learned on Leyte was what was important to carry. Of course the M-1 was the most important and then the shovel. I learned never to lay that down. When you got through using it you put it right back on your belt. I had a pair of suspenders down to my belt and on the back of those I had a sweater wrapped in my poncho tied on with a tent rope. I had a spoon in my pocket and I threw away my mess kit. It made too much noise. Every time you hit the ground in a hurry the gas mask would poke you in the kidneys so I got rid of that too, and even my bayonet. My can opener, canteen cup and canteen stayed with me. The lighter you were, the better off you were.

Having that bayonet on was dangerous. Crawling around in the mud at night you might just poke the guy ahead of you in the butt, which happened a few times. It made the rifle more clumsy to carry too, and would catch on the brush you went through. One guy even slashed his own knee with his bayonet when he jumped in his hole to avoid an incoming shell. I think our guys got hurt more by their own bayonets than they ever hurt the Japs.

The sergeant asked me what I was going to do when I ran out of shells and didn't have my bayonet on. I said I was just going back to look for more shells cause I didn't plan on doing any bayonet fighting. I'd always try to carry extra shells instead.

March 18, 1945

"Have you received the Jap watch yet? It should get there pretty soon unless it is like my Christmas presents."

"The news sounds pretty good now, but it looks to me like there is a lot of war left yet."

"Mrs. Otha Howell wrote me a letter the other day and said how sorry she was that I was wounded again."

"How is Robert coming along in school now? Say what grade is Mildred and Katherine in now? I can't keep up with them anymore. Seems like I have so much to think about I forget which grades and how old the kids are."

Okinawa

Late March of 1945 found us back on the troopships headed for Okinawa. The Japs had invaded the other islands we had been on, but Okinawa was their island to begin with, so we knew it was going to be different and a lot rougher.

When we arrived off the island our ships were all over the place, really stacked up. Our airplanes had dropped leaflets on the island telling the civilians we were coming and what they were supposed to do.

Before we landed the navy worked over the beachhead good, really pulverizing things. The Japs had pulled back and let us land so things were not bad at all. During the day my platoon made it up on a hill overlooking the beachhead, and we were busy digging in for the night. Once I had my hole dug I started getting rid of the equipment I didn't need so I could again travel light and fast. The gas mask, mess kit, bayonet and other pack items were discarded in a pile.

Suddenly, just before dark, low along the shoreline came seven Jap airplanes. They swerved out away from the shore and started attacking our ships which were just off the island. They were dropping bombs on the ships, and one bomb hit a ship and exploded, starting it on fire. The navy started cutting loose firepower to defend itself, and that was a little dangerous for us because a lot of time the aircraft were between us and the ships, and the navy shells would land in our area. It's a wonder the navy didn't shoot their own ships too, cause sometimes the airplanes were between the ships too. We sat up on the hill watching the whole battle. One Jap airplane might have been hit, I don't know. He came off a diving attack, circled back over shore, then headed back out and ran right into the side of a ship. The ship blew up and burned half the night before it sank.

Before we landed, they told us not to take any prisoners for two days. They would have no stockades or any place to put prisoners, so we weren't to take any. They didn't say what we were supposed to do with them, but seeing that anything that moved at night was to be shot, there wasn't much question as to what we were expected to do. The leaflets they dropped supposedly warned the people to stay away from our lines for two days. The papers were scattered all over the shore, but I couldn't read them as they were in Japanese. I was the assistant squad leader now, and just before dark this older-looking lady came walking up towards our line. I told this other guy in my squad, "Shoot her." He looked over at me and said, "I ain't gonna shoot her, you shoot her." My reply was, "I ain't gonna shoot her either." We got her attention, and motioned her away. She headed back in the opposite direction, and we didn't see her again, or know what ever happened to her. It was a dumb deal, she acted like she was in shock.

Another outfit was securing a road not far from us. Someone came down the road after dark and the boys opened up. It happened to be two women, who were both killed, but one had a baby on her back and it wasn't. That baby cried and cried. It sounded like a goat bawling, and made you really feel weird. Finally the shooting started again and there was no more crying. That was really bad, and hurt us all to have to do that. The next morning I saw the two women, and the baby in the backpack lying there. It was a bad deal to have to kill like that. The leaflets were supposed to have warned them. This was a Jap island and we found out they all were going to fight us, including the women and children. It was them or us, and we thought it was better if it was them.

Our tanks started to move down the road that morning, but were stopped when a young boy with a box of TNT jumped out of the ditch where he had been hiding, and put himself and the charge under the tank. He did a good job knocking out the tank. It blew the track apart and oil started running out of the bottom, but it didn't catch on fire. The tank guys weren't killed, just suffering from the concussion of the explosion. Blood was dripping from their ears and eyes. The boy with the TNT didn't look older than about twelve years.

The second day we didn't see many Japs. They all had vacated their homes and obviously knew we were coming because behind each house they had dug a big hole about eight to ten feet deep and six feet across for their personal belongings. I guess they figured their valuables would be better protected from fire or explosion in the holes than in their houses.

On the third day we saw a lot of Japs. One Jap was hidden in the ground and when the 1st Squad was almost on top of him, he jumped up with a machine gun and shot as many of them as he could before they could react and kill him. He didn't kill any, but he hit more than half of them. One of the guys came over by me, and he had been shot through the face. The bullet had entered in one cheek, and out the other with lots of blood just running out of his mouth. His shirt was soaked with blood. I don't know how much damage was done but it didn't look very nice with all the blood. He went back and I don't know how he came out as I didn't see him again.

Just beyond where the 1st Squad had gotten it there was a ridge. As the rest of the squad came up I looked over the top and saw Japs to the left. I picked off one and shot five more times as they dove for their holes. I couldn't tell whether I hit any more or not. Seconds later they shot a mortar round back which was close, but short. Two more rounds followed, but they hit shorter yet. I laid there for awhile, and pretty soon they came out of their holes again and I got one, maybe more before they were back in their holes. They shot a lot more mortar shells at us and my sergeant told me not to bother them anymore or we'd get some of our men hurt. We weren't going that way so we just bypassed them to the right.

The Japs had planned for our arrival for a long time. They had large eight-foot board crosses marking each hill and a map of the distance to each hill so when they knew where we were, it didn't take a lot of adjustment to zero in with the artillery and mortar shells. In the past we had artillery superiority, but here the Japs had us out gunned.

Many times they would wait until we were in the valley between two hills before they hit us. You could hear the guns go off behind the hills. They might fire a dozen times before anything hit, but you knew that after the first explosion there would be a lot more to follow. They liked to start the mortar rounds behind you about 25 yards apart and just walk them over you. That happened four or five times each day. There would be calm for 30 minutes, maybe even a couple hours, then they would start again. All we could do was lie in a hole and hope our name wasn't on one of them. Sometimes we were lucky and no one got hurt, but over a period of time they did get lots of our men that way. Our men would fire mortars back, but we didn't know exactly where they were, and if we did it would take two or three rounds to get the range. By that time the Japs would have moved. They did the same thing with their machine guns. After firing they would move back 150 yards or so, and do it all over again. Our boys were alert and would hit the dirt as soon as one opened up rather than looking to see where the bullets were coming from. That reaction saved a lot of lives from both the mortar and guns. Nevertheless the Japs were taking their toll. We were losing more men than we had in any other battle.

Early one morning two of our boys were eating behind a ridge when a mortar shell came in and hit right beside them. One was killed outright. The other ran in a circle ending up where he had started, and died. The mortar hit so close that it burned the boy's web belt. I guess that boy's luck had run out. He was the only other survivor of the duck that went down in Hawaii. He was the one that helped me pull that other boy from the water.

Well, we laid the two boys out side by side to get picked up, and meanwhile the squad sergeant and another guy went up to the top of this little hill to see how we would move out that morning. They were on opposite sides of a tree at the top of the hill when a knee mortar hit the tree about two feet above their heads. We ran up the hill to help them, but the sergeant was already dead. I helped the guy they called Pop haul the other boy down. He said, "Pop, don't let me die. I don't want to die." I could see many holes in his shirt and he had already vomited on it, so I knew he was going to die. Vomiting was a bad sign for stomach wounds. Now we had four boys dead and hadn't even seen a Jap that morning yet.

These knee mortars the Japs had were really quite a weapon. Certainly better than the ones we had. It was real portable and light, weighing about the same as an M-1 rifle. It didn't have a plate fixed to the bottom and was about the size of a two-inch pipe. It had a screw jack type of arrangement so you could increase or decrease the barrel depth to vary the range. It had a level bubble on the side and after you put the shell in, it didn't fire until you pulled a string to fire it off. It was accurate out to 400 or 500 yards and had about the same destructive power as a hand grenade.

Later that day we waited at the bottom of a hill with the 1st Platoon, while our artillery shelled the top. At a predetermined time the artillery intentionally started firing a little long while we headed up the hill to catch the Japs in their holes. That three or four minutes was critical. The Japs would still hear the artillery, but would not realize that it was being intentionally aimed past them. While we scrambled up the hill they still had their heads down. That worked pretty well most of the time. The 1st Platoon leader, a lieutenant, was close to me after an artillery shell went off, and he just sat there looking distant. He finally opened his mouth to say something, but couldn't, then fell over dead. It looked like the shrapnel had hit close to his heart. He was a nice guy and everybody liked him, it was sad.

I saw five of our tanks come over a hill and four were hit right away and when the other headed back a shell hit right where he had been. Over there I didn't even want a tank close to me because the Japs would shoot everything at them. They would have some of this artillery hidden in caves and they would wheel it out when they needed it, and blast away. The further those tanks were from me, the better I liked it.

The battle was one hill after another. Once we were pinned down by mortar fire all day. Towards night I saw a bunch of Japs heading out, up towards another hill. I really unloaded at them with the BAR and M-1. Whether I hit any, I don't know, but it felt good to send some back after taking it all day.

Between two hills we had to pass through a 20-yard open area. We went two men at a time and the Japs really poured it to us. Later we had to return back through the same area but no one got hurt either time. We sure were lucky, but aside from luck we had to work as a team to survive.

There was an old castle-like building we had to take. I was the first one up there and found a door laying outside with a pretty blanket on it. Maybe they had used it to carry wounded Japs, I didn't know, but it didn't look right laying out there in the road. I told the others not to walk on it or move it, which was a good thing, because later they discovered a mine underneath. The Japs had used the old castle for their dead and wounded. There were still some dead ones inside.

At the bottom of the hill below the castle, we set up for the night. As we were digging in two women and a boy came up and tried to throw a grenade at our machine gun. The boys killed them all and we had no one hurt that time.

We would find the women in the holes with the Jap soldiers. When they came out it was hard to keep from killing them too. Life is so dear that you have to shoot first and then check to see what it was that was killed. It is you or them. If you are killed, you are dead for a long time. We weren't over there to kill civilians, but it was hard not to when they stayed right with the soldiers.

Our squad cleaned out a tunnel getting everyone inside, except afterwards we heard a baby cry. At first we couldn't find out where he was, but finally found him lying in a well where his mother had probably laid him before she was killed. We took him back to an aid station. He had a small wound on his hand which looked infected.

The hills seemed to get worse. The Japs had years to prepare and there were trenches around the tops of the hills and tunnels all the way through. As much as they shot at us we thought they would be running short of ammunition, however we would find cement embankments loaded head-high with cases of it. I think we would have shot every shell rather than let them get a supply that large. We made sure they never got it back either by blowing it up or by burying it.

The Japs seemed to get thicker each day and harder to fight. We had a town to take and that was a new and dangerous experience. It was sure a lot different than the grass huts in Leyte. These people had streets with inlaid stone, gutters along the streets and sidewalks. Between the road and the home yards was a high wall, maybe seven feet or so, made out of sandstone blocks. Inside the wall about six feet was another wall. The entrances to the walls were not aligned, so you could not just go straight through to the house. You had to turn right or left and expose yourself. A grenade would help clean things out, but it was still dangerous because you weren't sure where they were. One house was vacant so I took a little time to rummage through the things that were left. I found some Chinese coins and a kimono which I packed up to take home. I tried on a Jap shirt but it was so small it ripped right up the back when I got it on.

On one end of the town the Japs had a rock barricade set up. They would fire down the main street and the sound of those machine gun bullets ricochetting off the walls was really weird. Towards evening they abandoned their strong point and you could see them running up the hill out of town. We sent a lot of raw lead after them. Some we must have hit, but we didn't go check. We were headed in a different direction. They didn't seem to want to fight at night. All day they would go at it, but when evening came they left. That was better for us, we didn't mind at all.

When we took the hills the tanks couldn't help us much because the Japs had big artillery and would knock them out. In fact the tanks were about useless. We had to rely on our own artillery to beat up the hill before we started up. This one day our artillery had shot so many shells at this hill you would think everything would have been dead. At the top though, there was a horse tied to a tree. He had been hit so many times with shrapnel, there was a blood trail out as far as the rope that held him would reach. It was hard to believe that he could be alive, but he was on his feet.

From the top of the hill I could see the Japs heading down the other side and I started shooting at them. The Jap artillery really started opening up on us now and the captain decided to pull the men off the hill until things cooled down. He left my squad up on the hill so that if the Japs tried to retake the hill we could radio down and tell him, and he'd bring the men back up to fight them.

Out of a squad of twelve men there were only five left in mine. The squad leader and his assistant had both been killed so I was the squad leader now. We took cover in an Okinawan burial cave, and took turns every few minutes to check and see if the Japs were coming up the hill. The caves were about seven or eight feet high with ledges where they laid their dead. The way I understood it, when the bodies decomposed they would put the bones in big vases. The entrance to the cave was only about three feet or so across, and it was marked by a stone on the outside. The opening to the cave was on the backside of the hill so if the artillery shell didn't hit right on the top of the hill it would have enough of an arc left to just go down to the bottom of the hill. Mortar shells were different, with a higher trajectory, so they would hit the backside of the hills. Sometimes the artillery shells were duds and made a special, "whoosh, whoosh," sound as they went by. They still were dangerous, like a booby trap, cause if they were disturbed just right they could go off. As I said we took turns looking for Japs coming up the hill and this one guy had just crawled through the opening to check when he heard an artillery shell coming in. You only have a couple of seconds to react after you hear them, so he dove headfirst back into the cave. It was a good eight or ten feet to the bottom of the cave and the artillery shell had hit about where he had been standing, so I didn't know whether he had been hit or not. He got up OK, but his nerves were now shot. Battle fatigue I guess. He couldn't hold his gun or anything and I tried to straighten him out, but I couldn't. Finally I sent him back down to the medics, and I had three men left.

I had seen shell shock and battle fatigue before. Wounds would heal, but I wondered if these guys would ever be the same. Their eyes would be out of focus with a staring look, and they weren't able to protect themselves other than to jump in a hole and hide. It's sad to see men this way. I've visited them in the hospital, and once when a guy sweeping the floor dropped his broom, they all dove for cover. Some they have to keep in rooms with bars on the windows.

We managed to hold the hill that day and the Japs didn't try to retake it. There had been so many hills and we knew there would be more. We were really hurt now, our numbers were down. Probably half our company was gone. They kept promising replacements, but none arrived. Just because we were operating with half a platoon or half a squad, we still were supposed to do the job of a whole one. If the Japs had known how bad they had hurt us, they could have run right over us. We had to go on though, because there wasn't anyone else to do it.

Later that day, we had to come by the spot where the squad sergeant and other three men were killed by the mortar. They were still lying there as we had left them, lined up and covered with a poncho. If I hadn't known who they were, I wouldn't have recognized them. Their faces were all dark and they had lost all their natural features. I didn't know how long it took to take care of the dead, but I was surprised it had taken that long. It had been four or five days since they had been killed. I felt bad about that. It was a good thing it was cool, in the 40s and 50s, or the bodies would have decomposed.

The Ninth of April found us trying to take a hill as bad as it was high. We had the artillery pounding it pretty heavy, and when the time came for the artillery to raise up and fire long, we scrambled up to the top. Hopefully we would catch the Japs in their holes and shoot them before they got their heads up. At the top I could see the Japs heading down the other side and I sent 20 or 30 rounds after them.

As soon as we took a hill the Japs almost immediately started shelling us. At the top of this hill the Okinawans had built garden plots the size of small houses, separated by trenches. A foot-wide raised path led along the gardens, and when I heard a shell coming in I jumped from the path into one of the trenches. The shell hit close right behind me. I think it must have been from our artillery and either they hadn't raised the gun up enough, or it was a short round, which happened occasionally. This shell hit so close behind me I could reach over and put my hand in the hole. The garden was soft and the shell went deep before it blew, but it still threw some shrapnel in my left shoulder, and drove dirt in the back of my neck. My neck burned and hurt so bad I thought it must be a really bad wound, and it was several seconds before I dared to put my hand back there and check. When I did, there was some blood where the sand had been forced in. The other boys in my squad thought I had really got it bad, because it had hit so close. They sent me back to the aid station where the medics cleaned up my neck and put a bandage on it. They said that the two pieces of shrapnel in my shoulder would be too hard to find so they just sent me back up to the front. The boys were surprised to see me back. The only thing that saved me was that soft dirt that let the shell go deep.

We spent the night on the top of the hill where I had been hit, and the next morning we moved out to take another. The Japs really gave us hell again, and when we reached the top of that hill there were several dead Japs and horses laying there that the artillery had gotten. That afternoon we moved to the backside of the hill so the Jap artillery wouldn't get us. We had just started to set up when a Jap mortar shell hit behind us and pinkish smoke came up. It was a smoke shell. The Japs used them to adjust their fire so we knew they would be putting more rounds on us soon. They told us to dig in for a mortar attack. Me and this other guy were feverishly working on the same hole facing away from the hill. I was on my knees digging and he was digging in the opposite direction. A mortar shell hit in front of me and I was hit in the chest. I don't remember much pain. It felt like someone had hit me hard in the chest with their fist, and then a numbing feeling. I looked at my fatigue shirt and there was a pretty good hole through it right above my heart. "I'm hit!" I yelled. The medic came over and put wide tape over the hole in my chest where the blood was coming out. That would help seal the hole so my lung wouldn't collapse. They took me on a stretcher back to the aid station. There they left the tape over the wound and just loaded me onto a jeep which headed for the base hospital.

The hospital was just a few tents put together. In the first tent they did some x-rays on me, and then I was moved to the floor of another tent. There they had a wounded guy on the table and two guys dressed in white uniforms stood beside him. I didn't know whether they were cooks or doctors. Finally they took the one guy off the table and put me in the stretcher up on it. The one guy in white started talking to me, "We don't think we can give you an anesthetic. You guys are too fatigued from combat. That other guy there we put out, and he quit breathing on us three times. Would you let us do it without anesthetic? It would be a lot better." "Well, go ahead and try to take it out," I said.

They tried to freeze the outside of the wound, but that didn't stop the pain. The shrapnel was too deep. They had a towel over my face and I grabbed hard on both sides of that old stretcher. The one guy started prodding around in my chest until he finally hit something. "I think that's it. You try and see," he said to the other. "Yeah that's it," was the reply. In no time at all they had the shrapnel out and laid it on a piece of gauze beside me. "Here you can take it home with you." It was a pretty good-sized chunk lying there.

I found out later that the same shell that got me wounded my captain and killed the lead machine gunner. Other mortar shells in that attack killed several more boys in my company too. We just didn't have time to dig in before they hit us, and there was no natural cover available to us.

April 11, 1945

Dear Mother and all — "Say, bet you are glad to hear from me again, for I know it would be swell to hear a line or two from you. Well I am on Okinawa Island and that isn't good. Now here is the bad news, or good news whatever you call it. I just got wounded again last night. It hit me in the left chest, but it isn't very bad. They have taken the shrapnel out already. My left arm is a little sore and they have it tied up so it is hard to write. Day before yesterday I was hit just a little, but they sent me back up to the front again and yesterday I got it. I don't know yet where I will go or what will happen to me. So don't worry about me."

April 18, 1945

"My chest is coming along swell and you need not worry about me like you are doing, I bet. I don't know what hospital I will go to yet. I should get to see Ralph Leland if I stay here very long. Boy I really have been lucky in this war so far."

Saipan

148th GENERAL HOSPITAL
APO 244
SAN FRANCISCO CALIF
DEAR MRS. HEPPE
   I WISH TO INFORM YOU THAT ON 20 APRIL 1945
YOUR SON PFC VERNON W. HEPPE 36407413USA
WAS MAKING NORMAL IMPROVEMENT. SHELL
FRAGMENT WOUND OF THE LEFT CHEST.
   JOHN W. BARR
   1st LT MAC REGISTRAR
April 23, 1945
   "Guess you thought that I wasn't ever going to write you
again, didn't you?"
   "I am coming along swell and you needn't worry at all. It
will just take a little time and they will have me as good as
new again. It doesn't hurt much anymore and my left arm is
OK too."
   "They took the piece of shrapnel out and I still have it.
Looks like an old plow point which we sold the iron man
about six years ago. Ha, Ha. It is about the same size as the
one I sent home before, maybe just a little bigger."
   "I go to the show every night and there are some boys here
that I know and can talk to. I have read a lot of books, but I
wish it was letters. My mail will be held up like last time,
only worse I guess."
   "Ralph Leland came up to see me yesterday and he stayed
all day. We had a swell talk. It seems like we both have a hard

time remembering some people back home. The names seem to have slipped our minds. Maybe we have been away too long."

"I am in the 148th General Hospital in the Mariana Islands. The weather here isn't too bad. It is warm days and cool nights with some rain. On Okinawa it was really cold at night and some days when the sun was out it was warm."

"This time I was wounded before the end of the battle, but on Leyte I went through the whole thing and then was hit."

"I was hit on the 9th of April too, but it was only a couple little pieces and I went back to the front, but the 10th of April it was too much. I was digging in at the time I was hit. The shells were falling all around me at the time, but I was lucky it wasn't any worse."

April 27, 1945

"Boy are they giving me hell now. I get a shot in my arm every three hours and that isn't good, and to top that off they sewed my wound up two days ago and I haven't been able to move since. It hurts more now than before, but it soon will be all right."

"I go to the show every night, but since they sewed me up I have to really take it slow."

"I had some ice cream yesterday and it was really good. Eats here could be better, but they are better than in New Guinea."

April 28, 1945

"Say Mother, I have a new address now, and I want you to write me as soon as you get it. Tell me if you got those things I sent home, like my watch and that Silver Star."

"We don't have much to do over here. I go to the show every night which for a change is pretty good. Most army shows are old and not much good. I have read most all the books we have here."

"I have been playing a lot of cards too. I have seen a couple of the boys in Snyder's company and we talked over old times."

"We live in a pretty good ward, but they have tin roofs on them and are really warm."

"They have a Red Cross here and girls come around most every day to see what the boys want. They have a PX here too and they do have a few things to sell in it."

"Say did they do any fishing in the river this spring? Boy, that is one thing I would like to do, and the other is to shoot some more pheasants in front of Jake again."

May 4, 1945

"I am about ready to leave the hospital. They told me this morning that it would only be a couple days before I left. I will go to another rest camp but they might try to make me work a little and I wouldn't like that."

"I sent home a package today and it is something like a housecoat which I got on Okinawa."

"I must close for this time as there just isn't anything to write about."

May 9, 1945

"Thought it was about time I wrote the old man a letter so here it comes and hope you like it. Seems like I can't write anymore like I could once. My mind just doesn't seem to go in for letter writing lately. If I could get a letter from you, why then it wouldn't be so bad. I worry over you at home and you worry over me. You needn't worry about me as what is to be will be that way if you worry or not."

"I am beginning to think that I am too mean for the Japs to get, but they sure as hell have been trying their best, and they aren't bad either. They have even had me wondering a couple of times. Boy if I ever get home I could tell you some things that would make you come right out of your chair."

"I have moved over to a convalescent hospital now and it won't be too long before I go back to duty again. I really want to go back this time for there are a lot of things which I want to even up on. You know this last island was their homeland and it is the place where we can kind of even things up with those yellow rats."

"Say what does Mother think of me getting hit so much? The day before I was hit in the chest I got a couple of small pieces in my back and some dirt blew in my neck. A shell hit about 10 feet behind me and if I hadn't had my nose in the dirt it would have killed me for sure. I thought it had anyway for a minute. I still have the one piece in my back, but it doesn't hurt any. My neck is OK too. That piece from Leyte is still in the front of my neck yet."

"Guess it is about time I said good-by, and Dad be sure to answer this letter because I will be looking for it."

"P.S. Elrena is having a birthday tomorrow and she will be 21 years old. Remember when I was 21? I do because it was just when I thought I had become a man. If I was a man then, I must be a grandpa now. Ha, Ha."

May 13, 1945

"I guess this is one day every guy should write home and tell his mother hello, and how much he really misses her and how much she means to him. I have thought a lot about you since I have been in the army and I couldn't ever see where I could have had a better mother than what you are. You are tops with me and don't let anyone tell you different."

"Well I hit it last night. My mail came in and there were 81 letters in all and that is a lot of them. There were letters from you which you wrote last December 10th. I received some convalescent cards for the wounds on Leyte and they at least got here in time for this wound anyway. I haven't read all the letters yet, but I have read all the ones you, Dad and Harvey wrote."

"I was glad you liked the Silver Star, as it is a pretty medal and maybe someday I will tell you how I got it. Not by letter though, as you would put it in the newspaper maybe. I don't want you to put any more of my letters in the paper. Don't feel bad about it, but it is something I don't want. It makes a guy look like a USO hero and God knows I have been through enough that I don't have to be one of them. The more people know, the more they will ask about when they get me cornered after I get home. We will just forget about what has happened in the past and look at life before us which I hope is really bright."

"Now I wish you many Happy Mother's Days to come and don't worry about me as I am just as good as when I came in."
May 15, 1945

"When I got the Silver Star the general of our division pinned it on my shirt and they took pictures, but I couldn't get any at that time. It was just before we left for Okinawa and we were really busy then. The general even shook hands with me."

"We have lots of butter now and I eat more here than at home. We also have lots of canned cream too. I would like more fresh eggs and some apples again."

"The fighting on Okinawa was the worst I ever saw in my life. Even the civilians were fighting and getting hurt too."
Sad word came from home. My old dog Jake had died.
May 16, 1945

"So you think that new dog will be as good as what Jake was? I don't think any dog could ever take his place. Not in my heart anyway. He would hunt anything that I wanted to hunt, and he was nobody's fool either when it came to hunting."

"Say, I see in one of your letters where you expect me to be home in six months. How do you get that? Before we went to Okinawa I tried for a furlough and even went up to see the colonel of our outfit, but it was no. There are lots of boys with more time over here and more battles too."

"Tell Robert not to come over here to help me because I don't want any of my brothers in this war."

"Say Harvey, what makes you think that Elrena is the girl for me? I haven't even made up my mind to get married yet, or even pick out the girl. It would be kind of hard to find a nice girl like you did, because nowadays they all spend more money on clothes in four months than I make in a year."
May 18, 1945

"I will be leaving here in a couple days so I will send you my new address then."

"So you really think I should get out now? Well I hope you are right about it. I asked the doctor and he said if you are fit, then back you go."

"Mother, I want you to quit having those dreams at night. They are the things that are getting me in trouble over here. Ha, Ha. I haven't had a dream for years myself. If I get to thinking about the Japs it is hard for me to go to sleep, and some nights I think about them because it was at night when we had our worst fighting."

"My captain is over here in the hospital with me. He was in the second bed from me and we played cards a lot before he moved. He is a nice guy but he can't do anything. I was happy to find he hadn't been killed.

May 21, 1945

"Harvey, have you got that new car of yours yet? You will really have a lot of girls after you then."

"Those boys sure are getting a lot of furloughs back home. Wish I could get one myself. I have left the hospital and am back to duty. I am waiting to go back to my old company again. I am about as good as before and know just a little more maybe."

MRS. ELIZABETH HEPPE

I WISH TO INFORM YOU THAT ON 21 MAY 1945 YOUR SON, PFC VERNON W. HEPPE, 36407431 WAS RETURNED TO DUTY* FINAL REPORT

EDWARD H. SEIFERT

COLONEL, M.C.

COMMANDING

May 26, 1945

"I am back to the hospital today, but only to see some of the boys. Most of them have been moved or shipped out. There were a couple of them left. There just isn't anything over here to do now."

"So you think that I should come home. There isn't anything I would like better."

"Haven't heard from anyone this last week. Guess I move around too much for my mail to catch up to me."

"I have been working the last three days at camp. They really are putting me on the ball now. Making me earn my meals anyway. If they don't get better I won't have to work hard for what they are worth. The hospital food is the best of all."

"Harvey asked me once why I wasn't a sergeant. Say, ask him if he would rather have me a PFC and come home or make sergeant. That is about the way it adds up over here. I was taking a sergeant's place last time when I was hit. It isn't worth it. Not in the infantry anyway."

"Well how is old brother Harvey coming along now? Hope you are keeping those girls happy back home. Ha, Ha. I received some mail today and was sure happy to hear from you. There were five letters in the bunch from you."

"Say you will have a nice 40 acres if you get those trees all cleared up, and it shouldn't take over a year. Bet if I was home we could clean it up fast."

"Harvey, I thought you said you had tires on that truck. Why are you buying new ones now? You will have a lot of money in that truck before long. If I should get out of the army can I drive it? Maybe Dad will let me drive his."

"Now you asked about me getting out of the army. I might get out, I don't know yet. I only have 82 points as they haven't counted any from Okinawa yet."

"Say, can a soldier buy a new car now? I will need a car, and if a new one isn't too high I will take it."

"Harvey, I would do almost anything to get home, so if I should get a chance to come home don't worry I will take it. That's what I have been fighting for, and it was worth it too if they let me go now."

June 2, 1945

"This month will be the start of the rainy season. Our tent seems to leak a lot and to make it worse it is right over my bed. Every island I have been on has been right in the rainy season except Okinawa. We were just ahead of it there."

"I was over to see Ralph Leland this week and we had a good old talk. It was about everything most of the time, but it would get back to girls every now and then. I never did see where six soldiers ever got together unless one of them was talking about women."

"Mother, I will tell you something now but don't let it worry you. On Leyte I was hit pretty hard in the neck, but it is OK now. It hit me in the blood vein in my neck and they gave me a pint and a half of blood. The doctor said afterwards that when I first came in he didn't think I would make it, but he didn't know me. I knew I would make it all the time and told him so."

"I have seen a lot of the boys down here that I know. I went to the hospital to see a couple from my squad."

June 5, 1945

"I am working at the hospital now as they are short of men. I was carrying wounded men around yesterday."

"I have 87 points now and should have at least five more before long. They still can change it so don't look for me before I get there."

"I bet you are looking for me to come home most every day now. Well you had better wait six months, and then start looking. I'll be lucky to make it by hunting season."

June 11, 1945

"Mother, you asked how I got the bola knife on Leyte? I traded a pair of pants for it."

"I think maybe I will have to get 250 chickens when I get home. Who knows, I don't know what I want."

"We get the news every day over here. They also have some radios around that we hear too. They print a paper every day and our division even printed a news sheet which we got up on the front lines."

"I hope it isn't too long before I find out if I am going to get out."

June 12, 1945

"Harvey, if you buy a new car can I drive it around just a little?"

"Better wait until I get there before you buzz up that wood. You could use the help and I need a little work to build me up. Haven't been doing much hard work since I was wounded."

"I am on guard duty every day now. I pull six hours every night. It seems like a long time. Haven't shot anyone yet."

"Say, how many cords of wood do you think you and I could put up in a day if Dad pulled them out with the tractor? I think we could get 30 a day if you could hold up on your end of the saw. Maybe even more."

"Say, can Robert do much yet? Guess he has too much lead in his ass to do much work around home. When I get back I will kick some of it out if he doesn't move around pretty fast. Ha, Ha. P.S., be sure to read this to him."

"Can you get lots of shells this year for the shotguns? Might need them if they will hurry and send me back to the U.S.A."

They came up with a point system that would allow soldiers to go home if they could qualify. I looked into it and applied. You had to have 85 points to leave. By this time I had a Purple Heart with three oak clusters, the Silver Star, four battles and two years overseas. That gave me 97 points and I could go home. The only thing I needed was a ship to go home on, and that would take some time. In the meantime they put me in charge of a shift of men to guard the hospital. That didn't sound like too bad a deal. The hospital and nurses quarters had a fence around it, but there were still some Japs in the hills so they wanted it guarded. About the only time the Japs would come out was at night to get food.

The hospital guard duty wasn't too bad. One night we would guard it from six until twelve at night and the next time it would be from twelve until six in the morning. I had a mixture of men, from those going home to those just starting overseas. I wished that the new guys had not had live ammunition because they would see more Japs at night than there actually were.

One night one of these weirdos thought he saw something move. It was a pair of nurses slacks she had hung on the clothesline. When he told the slacks to halt the wind kept blowing them, so he laid down in the road and fired six times at them with his pistol. He didn't do any damage, but he sure scared the hell out of a lot of people. I felt like taking the guns away from some of them, cause they obviously didn't know how to use them.

The nurses quarters were real popular even in the daytime. There weren't many girls on the island and guys would drive around there in the daytime and hopefully catch some outside sunning themselves. The girls' social life was tightly regulated, and if a nurse or USO gal went out on a date, they had to sign out and be back in by 10 p.m. They also had to be accompanied by two men, not just one, and the men had to be armed. There had been one bad instance where a lieutenant had taken a nurse to the beach and a couple of guys tried to attack them, I guess. The lieutenant got a shot off, but the two guys killed him and the nurse. One of the guys finally turned himself in cause he had a head wound caused by the lieutenant's forty-five. That's how they found out who did it.

It was usually the officers who got to date the nurses and USO girls. When they brought them back from a date they would be hanging around outside giving the girls a few last-minute kisses. That's when I had the satisfaction of running them off. I'd say, "That's enough, you guys gotta leave." And they would have to leave. It was a time when I could tell the officers what to do and it made me feel good.

This one guy brought a USO gal back to the nurses quarters parking lot in his jeep. Somehow he leaned over to kiss her or whisper in her ear, and his carbine went off. I heard the girl holler something like, "That sure spoiled a perfect day." I watched him take the clip out of the gun, but I knew another bullet had been inserted in the chamber when the first one fired. He pointed the gun up in my direction to clear it and I shouted, "Don't pull the trigger, it's loaded?" I knew he would pull the trigger and I jumped for cover as it went off. Boy, if I could have gotten down there faster I would have gotten ahold of him, but he was on his way out in his jeep.

When we were in combat going from one island to the next, battle after battle, I knew I wouldn't make it. The fear was about gone, no need to worry about it. You could be lucky only so many times. They would bring some new men in to replace those that were killed or wounded and if you weren't too bad you got back just in time to go again. I heard later that out of the 199 men that we started out with on Okinawa, only 32 were left after 24 days. Things were different now. I had to play it close to the belt, as it would be a hell of a time to get killed just before I was to go home. It would be even worse to get shot by one of our guys cause he didn't know how to handle a gun.

They asked for some volunteers to go up in the hills and hunt Japs, but I wouldn't do that. I wanted to make it. I thought the hard part was over.

There were some funny things that happened while we were guarding the nurses quarters. It was real hot there and some nights the girls would have little parties in their quarters and go around inside without any clothes on. The fence that went around the building was about 40 feet from the buildings and at one point there was a gate which we had to have guarded. Well, I had two guys guarding the gate and they had a little something planned that night. I said, "I don't want to know anything about it. Don't get me involved cause I'm going home soon."

The nurses quarters had these double doors across from the gate where my boys were, and occasionally the wind would blow the doors open a little so they could see in. Well, they had a long string which they tied to the door to help the wind out a little. They would pull the door open some to see, and then a nurse would come over and pull it closed. This went on for quite awhile and I guess they finally got bored and went inside the gate to take the string off the door. Well some nurse inside heard them and started screaming. This guy really used his head though. He called halt three times, then fired a couple of shots in the air and hurried back to the gate. I was back at the day room when I heard the shots, and I said to myself, "Those guys really goofed up this time." I ran over there and they told me what happened. Pretty soon the captain of the guard showed up and asked what the shooting was all about. I said that the guards had seen someone around the nurses quarters and ordered him to halt which he didn't, so they had to shoot at him. Unfortunately, I said, "He got away." The nurses came out and confirmed the story. They had heard someone, and the guards had yelled halt and shot at him. Well it was a good thing it was dark out, otherwise the captain would have seen the grin on my face. He thought it would be a good idea if I took some men and searched through the bushes out there, so we pretended to search the area looking for the mystery intruder. I was hoping nobody would be out there or he'd really be in trouble. No one found out what really happened, and it really was a good part the nurses fault for running around without any clothes on anyway.

Saipan had B-29 bombers based there. A boy from back home was in the army air corps and one day we went out and watched them take off. The planes were loaded so heavy it took every ounce of power to get off. When they finally did get off they were really low for a long time. Sometimes they never did make it off for one reason or another, and then over the cliff they would go.

One night when I went to the movie the bombers were just starting to take off. They were leaving in 20-second intervals. There were so many of them that when I came out of the movie they were still going. The next morning we'd see them returning from their mission. Sometimes they would be pretty well shot up. Out of the four engines, they might have two or three running. I never did see one come back with only one engine going, so I guess if they were in that situation they didn't make it back. There was another island, Tinian, that was real close and you could see the bombers going and coming from their base too.

Every so often the hospital commander would throw a big party for the doctors and nurses and then somehow the curfew would be extended until 12 a.m. A nurse told me that she didn't want to go because she was married. I guess her husband was a captain or major in the marines. She said that when the colonel in charge of the hospital invited you, there was no choice, you had to go. I was in charge of the guard detail that night. One of the officers was tending bar, and had his own bottle behind the bar. He said he was allowed a fifth a month. Guess he felt sorry for me out there while the party was going on inside, so he slipped some drinks out. It still didn't seem fair they could get the curfew changed, because no one else could. When it was

12 I had to put pressure on them to shove off, otherwise they would never leave.

June 13, 1945

"Dad, I didn't want you to feel too bad about those letters you put in the newspaper. That is the past."

"Say, I will take a pup from you for $25 and you can take it out of the $50 that it cost you for the use of Jake. Ha, Ha."

"I sure would like to get that mail carrier's job at home. My years in the army would count on my time too."

"Guess you had better let me pick out that wife, because I think that it is a much harder job nowadays. I think it might be a lot of fun just to look around for a few years and see what is on the market. I don't want a pig in a bag. Ha, Ha."

"I have been on 14 islands in all, five of them up north. We stopped on two islands before we got to Leyte and that is where I got the seashells."

"Haven't heard a thing yet when I will get home. Hope it won't be too long. They just don't tell us a thing over here. We are waiting for a ship to take us, but I think they are still building it yet."

June 15, 1945

"Mother, yes I did forget about your birthday. I had thought of it before but when the time came it slipped my mind. I did have a lot on my mind about that time."

"No, I never saw the show, I'll Be Seeing You. I don't like to see war pictures myself, as they aren't like the real thing at all. Don't know why they let some of those shows even go out. I don't much care for shows anymore."

"I told you once not to send any more socks or clothes. I get them for nothing here, more than I want to carry. I have a big bag now full of new ones and new shoes too. What do I want with a hope chest? I only hope to get home soon."

"The general who gave me the Silver Star was our division general, and his name is Major General A.V. Arnold. It would be a nice picture to have, but I asked for one before we left for Okinawa and there weren't any. A general pinned the

Purple Heart on me, and he was a swell guy too. He had our division at that time and we all liked him."

June 21, 1945

"Say, I received those nuts the other day and they are really good. I have eaten a lot of them already."

"So you are glad that I am not married, and so am I. That is one thing I won't have to worry about. I won't be married until after the war is over."

"Maybe now I will be able to come home just like I left, that is a free man. My sergeant was killed the 7th of April and the boy who took his place was hit the morning of the 10th. It almost got me too that morning. Had me jumping pretty fast. It was really close, but I was in a hole so I wasn't hurt."

"I might send home some nice souvenirs, but the most important one is still over here yet, and that is me. Ha, Ha."

"They have counted the Okinawa battle now, so I should have 92 points and maybe the other five for being wounded twice on Okinawa. I am going to look it up someday now that my service record is here."

"If I come home I should get out at Fort Sheridan, Illinois. I haven't heard a thing since I last wrote you, but I wish they would hurry up and send me home. I still think I will make the hunting season, I hope."

June 22, 1945

"Hello Dad. Sure was glad to see that your arm is OK yet. Your letter was really swell and I won't forget it either."

"I was over to see Ralph Leland the other day. We talked over old times and girls. I ate dinner and supper with him. Say, there is another boy from Ionia in this hospital. His name is Orval Oyler."

"When I get home and Frank wants to sell his place I am going to buy it through the G.I. Bill."

"When I get out I will work at home for 30 days and cut wood. Maybe we can get most of it out then."

"Sure glad you looked into that job I asked you about. It would make almost everything OK if I could get it. How much does a game warden make?"

"I hope to make it by hunting season, and tell the boys that one round is all I need. After that they can start shooting. If they aren't as hard to kill as a Jap it won't take over one, but sometimes it takes five or six shots. The one I shot New Year's Day was hit three times in the head and he even tried to get up. They are like deer. The day before Christmas I shot three times at one and he went down every time, but would get back up again until the last time. At last on Leyte when we would run into a bunch of them they would throw away their rifles, hats and packs, then start running like hell. Just like running rabbits out of a hole. It was fun when they didn't shoot back. My company would get 20 or 30 most every day and we wouldn't even have one shot fired at us some days. Guess you are tired of the war so I won't write any more of this. I will tell you some of it when I get home."

"Say, you can have the quart as I don't drink myself. If I had it over here it would be worth $35, and beer is a dollar a can. It only costs 10 cents a can, but we only get six cans a week. I have seen these crazy soldiers give $24 for a case of beer. These damn sailors seem to have it all."

"I will have five months pay coming by the end of June. I still have money I won in a card game on Okinawa. Don't need much here."

June 26, 1945

"I am back to the replacement center now. They brought me back last Sunday. My mail has been pretty slow this last week. There just isn't much to write about from here."

July 2, 1945

"I am still at the same place, and it looks the same as a week ago. Hope they start moving us pretty soon. They haven't sent anyone from over here yet."

"I see you are getting the house all fixed up on the inside this summer. Guess you are making those boys and Dad do a little work around home. That will keep them from fishing too much. Ha, Ha."

"Say, tell Mildred her letter was swell and I hope to be home soon and see her. Ask her if she will go to the show with me then. I need a pretty girl to go. Ha, Ha."

"There are some Japs around here yet, but they don't hurt anything now. They live in the hills."

"Say those strawberries really sounded good, but let Harvey have my share this year and I will eat his next year. Haven't seen any of them for a long time."

"I have been working most every day over here. Last Saturday I was on KP again and it isn't very nice. I was on detail today also."

July 7, 1945

"Dear Mother and all—I received a letter from you yesterday so thought it would be nice to answer it right back. Haven't been writing very much lately."

"So Katherine doesn't like to work around the house very well. Where does she like to work at?"

"It has really been raining over here. Every day and night we get a couple good rains. The mud is bad too. The tent I am in now doesn't leak, so that helps some."

"So you are going to those picnics again this summer. Are there any good-looking girls that come to them? If there were I might like to go. That ice cream sounds good too."

"We have lots of sugar and butter, but not the eggs like you do. The eats could be worse I guess."

"So Mildred can remember the day I left home. Well I can too. Seems like it was 10 years ago since I left home. The day I got on that train I never dreamed that the road I was going on was going to be so long and far away. It won't be so bad if I get to go home now and get out of the army too. I should make it this time."

"Tell the boys that when I get home we will cut wood for a month or two."

"Haven't been getting much mail lately and don't think there is much to get now. Albert wrote me a letter the other day and he said it was hot out there too."

Your Loving Son
Vernon

It was the last of May when I got out of the hospital and found out I could go home, but it was July before a ship arrived to take me there. The ship came into the harbor and the captain said he could take 200 men to the USA. My name came up on the list of 200 and boy was I happy.

The food on the ship was great. It was really a slow-moving ship, but I didn't care, it was headed in the right direction. The other good thing about this trip was that the navy did all the work. There were no details for us. We just laid around and relaxed. My feet had never healed up. The athlete's foot problem was real bad, so I kept my feet out in the sun. They said that would help them heal.

We landed on the Hawaiian Islands again and they put us in a camp for a week. They went through our records and made sure everything was in order and that we had good uniforms to go back. They also made us dump our personal belongings out on a picnic table to make sure we weren't taking things from the war home. When they had examined everything, we had to repack it and put it into a big pile where a guy with a gun watched it. Probably the big reason for the guard was so the guys didn't sneak illegal stuff back in their bags.

I had a little time off to visit my friend that was stationed at Scofield Barracks. He had spent his whole overseas tour there. It sure was a lot safer than what I had been through.

Finally they had us load all our bags on the ship and we headed to America. The water was smooth and the weather fine. It was a slow journey, but peaceful. As we approached San Francisco Bay a big whale came alongside the ship. I had seen them blow before at sea, but had never seen one that close. He looked like a big submarine when he went by.

When we went under the Golden Gate Bridge you never saw a happier bunch of guys. A lot of us thought many times we'd never be home again, so it really was a big thing. But do you know what they did to us then? They didn't even let us go to shore. They took us out to Angel Island, which is by the prison island Alcatraz. That sure didn't go over very good with the boys. They had been overseas for two to four years and now they were stuck on an island and to top it off, the people that ran the island were Italian prisoners of war. Worse yet, the Italians could get passes to go to shore, but our boys who had been fighting the war couldn't.

As hard as all this was to take, I guess I realized that if they had let us go to shore, they never would have gotten us all back together for discharge. They went through our things again and checked all our clothes. I had a new pair of shoes that I had only worn on the boat from Hawaii, but they took those and all extra clothes and put them in a pile in the street and burned them. I couldn't understand that.

When they finally took us off the island and we landed on shore, there was a train waiting right by the docks to take us to Fort Sheridan in Illinois. It wasn't a real fast train, but the progress was steady until we got into some place in Iowa where we were delayed two hours while they cleared a wreck off the tracks ahead. There was a small town there, and a lot of the guys got off. They blew the whistle three times when they were ready to go, but there were a lot that weren't there when we pulled out. I could see a pickup truck racing along trying to catch up to the train, and moments after that we came to an abrupt halt. I didn't see what happened, but someone said later that the pickup truck had been trying to get close to the moving train so a soldier could jump back on. Apparently he fell under the train and it cut one or both his legs off. We were delayed another couple of hours while they investigated that. For the rest of the trip they wouldn't let anyone off when we stopped.

We finally reached Chicago and pulled into a huge rail yard at about six in the morning. They spent a half hour or more shifting the cars around to different tracks, and in the meantime a few boys slipped off and came back with a big bottle of liquor. We hadn't eaten in quite awhile, so it wasn't long before the liquor started taking effect. The ride to Fort Sheridan was a slow one, but the boys didn't care now. It was around noon when we got there and the boys were quite happy. They threw everybody's duffle bag out of the boxcar onto the ground and asked us to claim them. About 20 were unclaimed. I guess those were the boys that never made it back on when they slipped off the train out West.

Well we picked up our duffle bags and were herded into a small briefing room where a 1st lieutenant tried to give us a lecture. The boys weren't in much of a mood to listen and so they visited. This made the lieutenant real mad. He said that this was the worst lookin' bunch he had ever seen. He hadn't been overseas, and we weren't about to take that so we booed him so much he just gave up and left.

At Fort Sheridan they put us up in three-story cement barracks, and guess what? They had German prisoners of war wandering all over the place. They had PW on the back of their shirts, but walked around straight, tall and big-headed like they owned the place. Some of the boys had just gotten back from the war in Europe, and had buddies killed by Germans, maybe even these Germans. A pop bottle came down off the third floor and hit one right on the head and knocked him out. They took him to the hospital and then shortly thereafter the colonel had us in for a little visit. "I know it may not look nice to see these German prisoners walking around here, but they are doing the cooking, cleaning and all the rest of the work. If you hurt any more of them you boys will be taking over those chores." We didn't bother them after that, except we left the latrines and things good and dirty for them to clean. They didn't complain though, just walked tall and did the work. It still didn't seem right though. Some of our boys that got in trouble from returning to base late, and things like that, had to sweep the streets and dig ditches while the MPs watched them with guns. Meanwhile the Germans didn't seem to be watched at all. We booed the MPs.

We also didn't salute lieutenants that hadn't been overseas and didn't have any battle stars on their coats. I thought we'd get in trouble for that, but we didn't.

They went through all our records again and also provided our back pay. I hadn't been paid for over a year, but I just took a little cash and had them send the rest home in a check. They had a form for us to sign that said we were in just as good a shape as when we came in the army. If we signed it, we would be able to get home quicker. I wouldn't sign it cause I knew that would be a lie. I had been wounded four times and was not in the same shape as when I came in. They sent me over for the doctors to look at me. I heard one doctor say to another that it didn't look as if my chest had healed up very good. It was real sore, almost like a boil. The pain was there, even when just a shirt rubbed it. They looked me over some more and gave me some tests and finally my name appeared on the bulletin board list of those to be discharged. It was August 12, my Dad's birthday.

I rode the elevated electric train back down to the station in Chicago where we had passed a week before, and from there I got my train to Grand Rapids.

Coming Home

The train ride from Chicago to Grand Rapids seemed to go pretty fast. Guess I was just excited about getting home and seeing everyone. Dad didn't have a telephone yet, so I called Ed Peterson's place and asked them to tell Dad that I was in Grand Rapids and needed a ride home.

Ed came along to help Dad find his way to the train station, as Dad hadn't driven in Grand Rapids before. Dad's car had always been pretty reliable, but that night it chose to overheat about the time they were passing through Lowell. Ed called home and had his wife bring his car over so they could complete the other half of the trip to pick me up.

It was getting close to two in the morning and everybody else that had arrived on my train had been picked up. I was about the only one left in the train station, and was beginning to think nobody wanted me at home. It just wasn't the type of homecoming I had expected. My disappointment soon left when Dad and Ed pulled up to the station.

Everybody was still up when I got home, and boy were they happy to see me, and how they had changed. My little brother was not a little brother anymore. He was now a big brother. When the sun came up the next morning we were still talking. From November of Forty Two till August of Forty Five, I had been away from home, so we had a lot of catching up to do.

The war with Japan was over two days after I was discharged. When I was over in Saipan the airplane boys said that something big was going to happen and that the war would soon be over. Nobody believed them though, as we had just been going from island to island and I couldn't see any way that it could be over quick. They must have known something though, cause the rumor was out and the atomic bombs proved them right.

I was one of the first boys home from the war and boy was I popular. On Saturday night I wore my uniform into town and wherever I went people wanted to talk to me and buy me drinks. So many people seemed familiar, even though I didn't really know them. Everybody sure was nice to me and wherever I went my money just wasn't any good. Whether it was the Elks Club or the Moose, nobody would let me buy my own drinks.

This one girl named Kathleen came up with a couple girl friends and asked who I was, and where I had been. I said I had been wounded and came from a hospital on Saipan, and was there visiting another Ionia boy, Ralph Leland. Ralph had been on an antiaircraft artillery battery on Saipan. My name, picture and several articles had been in the Ionia County News, but a lot of people didn't know I was home. I didn't give the girl my name, so she went over to Lelands to find out who I was.

After that first Saturday I didn't wear my uniform anymore. In fact it seemed good to get out of it. Things had settled down and I was helping Dad on the farm. We were the only farmers for a long ways around to have a grain combine, and the work was really piling up. Dad had a list of folks waiting for him to come over with the combine and harvest their grain. Dad had hired another guy to work the combine with my brother Robert. During the middle of the day Dad and I would go over and keep it running while they ate lunch. We pulled it with Dad's tractor, but the Allis Chalmers combine had its own motor to operate the threshing process inside, and run the cutting bar which left a five-foot swath. It didn't have a grain bin though, so one guy had to stand on the combine platform and run the grain into bags. It seems like a lot of work now, but in those days it was a lot easier than cutting the grain and hauling it all up to the barn to run through a threshing machine. That took a lot longer and required lots more labor. Anyway, there was plenty of work for Dad's combine. After wheat came the oats and finally we'd combine clover seed.

When the war ended all the factories that had been putting out war goods just stopped their operations and laid the workers off. Those workers plus the boys coming home were all looking for jobs. This wasn't going to last too long, because with all the shortages during the war years people were ready to start buying things. It would just take awhile before the factories got switched over to producing what the people wanted. Along with the farm work at home I managed to pick up a few other extra jobs until the employment opportunities improved. I didn't have a car anymore. Harvey had wrecked my other car while I was in the service. Dad had an old Thirty Six Ford pickup and a Forty One Chevrolet, so I had those to borrow.

It was on Halloween that I saw that Kathleen girl again. She was walking downtown with her sister, and I asked if they wanted a ride. I had the old Ford pickup with a flat bed on the back, and eventually we had it loaded up with kids. Everybody was kinda wild it seemed, throwin' pumpkins out in the street and yelling a whole bunch. The cops didn't seem to mind though, as the kids weren't really destructive, just letting off steam. Everybody was happy the war was over. Later that Halloween evening I took Kathleen's sister home, and we just drove around town for awhile.

Several girls wrote me while I was in the army, but when I returned home it seemed like things had changed. Either they weren't interested anymore, or they didn't look that good. I took one of those girls out to dinner and she brought along her sister and her sister's boyfriend. I got stuck paying for the whole meal, so I didn't return to her house again. From the sound of her letters, the girl in Kansas had even changed. I did see Kathleen around occasionally. She was supposed to be going with some guy in the service and had a ring he had given her. The ring looked like glass to me, and not a diamond. Sometime after Christmas I asked her out and we went out on our first date. Unfortunately when I brought her back and pulled up in front of her house, Mr. Renucci, a neighbor, came running out and said she should go right in. Her mother had developed a blood clot and died. She hadn't been sick at all, so it was a real shock to the family. That put our romance on hold for quite awhile, but eventually in Forty Six we got together and started seeing each other on a regular basis.

Before I went into the army I worked at the Reed factory where they produced Jeep seats. When I returned I still held my seniority so when they started up in Forty Six, I was back at work in the factory. I made a dollar an hour, about the same as before I left. They were manufacturing wood station wagon bodies for Chevrolet and Pontiacs then. Although they never proved to be real popular in the long run, people were so anxious to be able to buy a car, they would take anything with wheels on it.

A year after the war was over things were still scarce. Manufacturing still hadn't caught up to demand. I ordered a small cedar chest for Kay's Christmas present, and every time I checked it still hadn't come in. My uncle used to make fun over that. He said, "I'll fix up a cigar box for her, that's good enough. You'll never get that cedar chest." Well, I did get the cedar chest, but in February or March.

My name had been on the list for a new car too. Just havin' your name on the list didn't mean you would get a car though. You really had to be there when the cars came in, otherwise some other guy would squeeze in ahead. More than once, when my name was high on the list, I would come in and find that the new shipment of cars had come and gone. Finally in March of Forty Seven I went into Breimayers and they said they had one car left. I didn't care what it was, I just took it and was happy. That summer of Forty Seven, Kay and I decided to get married. The wedding was on the 2nd of August, and certainly not a big one. It was just she and I, the preacher, and a couple that stood up with us. We took my new Chevrolet and headed to the Upper Peninsula of Michigan for our honeymoon. They didn't have nice motels in those days. We spent our first night in a little round-roofed building that looked like a chicken house. It worked just fine though, and started a happy marriage.

I had saved quite a bit of money while I was in the service and would liked to have bought a house. Houses were just not available though, for sale or for rent. We finally found this one old couple in Ionia that rented a whole house, lived in the downstairs, and re-rented out the upstairs bedrooms. It wasn't much, just three bedrooms with one entrance. We had to walk through the old folk's front room to get to our room. We had no cupboards or refrigerator. I made a box to keep things cool outside of the north window, and Dad gave us an old table from the basement to eat on. We used a washstand I had made to sit on. I had ordered a nice metal kitchen table and chairs, but like everything else, it took several back orders before it ever arrived.

We lived in the upstairs apartment for a year and then moved to another rental on Washington Street. I kept watching the newspaper for a house to buy, but every time one was advertised for sale, by the time we called it was sold. I think the realtor already had someone in mind when it became available. Seemed like kind of a dirty deal to me.

Kay and I were doing pretty good financially. I was making $1.25 an hour in the factory now. Out of each week's paycheck we'd plan 10 dollars for our rent, electric and the fuel bill. Ten dollars was used for food and another 10 dollars we used for leisure. The last 10 dollars went for savings.

On weekends I helped Dad, Harvey and Robert cut firewood to sell. Dad had sold the timber for 1200 dollars, but was making a lot more than that selling the treetops for firewood. There was a coal strike and a lot of demand for wood. Dad had the steel wheels on the tractor and would pull the tops out for us to trim and cut in lengths. We'd do that one weekend and then the next we'd run them through a buzz saw into eighteen-inch chunks. Dad sold one guy three hundred cords. The man had a dump truck and I believe his name was Hank Moon.

We had been living in the second rental for almost a year when we heard there might be a farm for sale out by Dad. The trouble was that it was really hard to find a way to finance a land purchase. That summer Kay and I took a little vacation down to Illinois. During the visit a cousin assured me that if I wanted to buy the farm, he'd loan me the rest of the money I needed. With that in mind I found out more about what it would take to buy the place.

The folks that owned the farm were the Petersons. They had lived there for 38 years and when Mr. Peterson died the old lady only lived on the farm in the summer and spent the winters in town. She rented the fields out and the house and barns had fallen into disrepair because nobody was around to look after them. There were 152 acres in the farm and they only wanted 13,000 dollars for it. I had always been quite a saver, so from what I had accumulated before, and during the service, I had 5000 dollars to put down on it. Unfortunately, my cousin changed his mind and would not back me. Even with my 5000 dollars to put down, the banks still turned me down on a mortgage for the rest. Since the depression they now had strict new rules for lending, and I didn't qualify. Being confident that I could obtain the financing I had put $200 down to hold the farm for 30 days. Now it looked like I might not get the farm and lose the $200 too. I asked a lot of individuals for help, but nobody had any money. Finally I approached the Yeomans family where we used to sell milk. They said they didn't have extra cash, but they heard that Ed Peterson's wife had inherited some cash and they might help out.

Ed Peterson was born on the farm I was trying to buy. I had worked for him before and established a good reputation. When I approached him for some help, he readily agreed to furnish the $8000 to complete the deal. I would pay him 5% interest plus $500 on the principal each year. I was already paying 25 dollars a month on the rental, so the money I'd save by not renting would almost make my interest payment.

Before I bought the farm, there had been only two other families living there, the Petersons and the Higbees. The Higbees had originally settled in the Belding area. After two years there, they were convinced that the railroad and good roads weren't coming in that direction, so they homesteaded this farm. This was one of the last farms in Ionia County that the government let out for homesteading. The farm was so wet that it didn't look too attractive for farming and was the last to go. The Petersons had used most of the farm for pasture and only a few fields to raise crops. Just before I bought the farm they put a big ditch through here that pretty well drained the land. It was a surprise to everyone that underneath that water was some excellent soil. I can remember as a kid I duck hunted in knee-deep water on the fields that now raise bumper crops.

Everything about the farm required a lot of hard work and money to get it in shape. The factory was only providing four days work each week then, so the rest of the time I was spending on the farm. I bought the old H Farmall tractor off Dad, and a two-bottom plow. The tractor didn't have any lights and could only be started with a hand crank, but it did give me a start at working the fields and for awhile the rest of the machinery I needed would have to be borrowed. The barn was in really bad shape, and before I could get many cattle it would have to be fixed up. I would come home from the factory at night and after supper Kay would shine the spotlight from the car on the barn for me to see, as I renailed the siding.

The house was almost as bad a shape as the barn. The window frames had rotted and I had to put in new ones. There was no bathroom or water inside. This was certainly a hardship on Kay who had been used to living in town. There was a windmill outside of the house, so if she wanted water to fill the 15 gallon crock in the kitchen she'd have to pull the steel lever outside and wait for the wind to come up. Sometimes she would be busy with something else when the windmill started pumping, so the crock would run over on the kitchen floor. Soon after we got there I did have a well and an electric pump put down in the basement to solve that problem.

The only heat in the house was a small oil heater in the floor of the living room. It was hardly big enough to heat one room, let alone that big house. I would come home at night from the factory and Kathleen would be lying on the only registered covered with a blanket trying to keep warm. There already was a chimney in the house, so I finally installed a big wood stove to get us through that first winter. The next year I had a combination coal and wood furnace installed with duct work throughout the house.

Those first years were certainly hard. It's a good thing we were young. We had accumulated very little, so about everything had to be purchased. From things as small as a hammer, to fertilizer and seed for the crops, plus all the regular living expenses. We were really in debt and the bills formed a large pile. Also on our first year at the farm I got Kay pregnant.

Dad gave me a cow and I purchased a heifer. Those were the only two cattle I had that first year, and it was a good thing because the barn needed too much work. In fact, there was no water in the barn. I had to lead the cow and heifer up to the house for a drink each day. I had a tub positioned outside the house that I pumped full of water from the basement.

The farm work got more difficult the next year when I bought more cattle. I normally would be out at the barn for milking by 4:40 a.m., and leave for the factory at 7 a.m. After work I'd milk the cows again, eat supper and start on the field work. I set a goal for my field work each night, and would work until I had reached the goal even if it was 11 p.m. Occasionally I would have to work overtime at the factory, and then Kay would milk the cows. Kay didn't care that much for milking. She said that when she went in the barn the cows would look at her as if to say, "What are you doing out here?"

When we had more cash I purchased a better tractor, a 350 Farmall with a three-bottom plow. I taught Kay how to plow and she accomplished a lot while I was working in the factory.

Kay had always lived in town before we met. She had been brought up in the town of Palo, until her family moved to Ionia when she was fourteen. The farm living wasn't easy and a lot more work than she had been used to, but she adapted quickly. She learned to do all kinds of field work and take care of the cattle while I was working in the factory. Even when I was home we'd be out together in the field working both tractors. I ruined her as a hired man that first year though, when I got her pregnant. After we had the oats planted she was sick a lot and couldn't do what she had before.

In the early years on the farm I didn't have enough time to get many crops planted in the spring. The factory was usually shut down for a couple months during the summer so I had time to work the ground and plant wheat then. Wheat was worth good money, and I tried to get at least 50 acres planted each year. In six years I had paid off the farm with the wheat harvest alone. I rented some of the land out to Harvey to begin with, and he planted corn in the spring. Eventually with Kay's help, I was able to get more corn and oats planted in the spring and I didn't raise as much wheat.

Carol was our firstborn in 1950 followed by Garald in two years, and eight years later came Jayne. When the kids got big enough to help they were all working alongside of Kay and myself, even little Jayne used to help unload bales of hay.

After several years of milking cows I decided that it wasn't returning enough income for all the labor we were putting into it. We changed over the barn and started raising beef calves into steers for market. That gave us a lot more flexibility in our life style. Milking the cows twice a day required a rigid schedule, and with me working in the factory it put an extra load on everybody. We still raised our own feed for the beef and the factory break in the summer allowed me plenty of time to put up the hay. The only big drawback to the beef operation was that the way the barns were set up all the manure had to be pitched by hand. Every Saturday my son Garald and I were cleaning the barn, pitching manure into the spreader. Garald always said I did a big favor for him in that respect, because it made up his mind that he never wanted to be a farmer.

Despite all the hard work, the farm turned out to be prosperous and something we were all proud of. At one time or another almost every room of our 100-year-old farmhouse had been remodeled. The barns had new windows and were repaired and painted. The wet fields that had only been used for pasture before now were productive and free of willow roots and the large rocks that had been there. In the meantime I continued to work full-time in the factory and each year received letters commending me for never being late or sick. I would have gladly swapped the congratulatory letters for some additional pay, but it didn't work that way.

In 1971 I went back to school and got my high school diploma. My mother asked why I wanted to do that, and I replied that it was one piece of paper that I just wanted to have for my own satisfaction.

For years and years I had told Kay I would really like to talk to some of the guys I had fought with from Company G. Finally I read in my veterans magazine of a 184th Infantry Regiment reunion, and I wrote to the guy in charge to see if I could get addresses of some of the men. Our daughter Carol was living in Portland, Oregon, so I thought maybe we could visit her and go on to California to see some of my old war friends too. I received the names and addresses of eight company men, and we set up the trip.

After visiting Carol we drove to see Uncle Albert. I tried phoning some of these guys on my list. The first guy I got a hold of thought I was kidding when I told him who I was. I didn't really remember the guy even though he was from my company, but he certainly didn't want to talk with me. Another guy I knew agreed to get together with me and go over my list of names. He pointed to several names and said I wouldn't want to contact them, they were either alcoholics or crazy. He didn't offer to go with me or to help locate the others. I got a hold of another guy and he agreed to meet me at his home at a certain time, but he never showed up. There wasn't any American Legion in the area to contact and I asked different people around if they remembered Company G, but nobody even heard of it. Twenty years had passed and the army had reorganized I guess. It was awful. I was the most disappointed guy you ever saw. For years I had looked forward to reconnecting that part of my life and now that I had the chance, it wouldn't happen. The memories were so bad nobody wanted to talk about it.

Years later Kay and I went to a veterans convention in Peoria, Illinois. A guy from Pewamo and another from Grand Rapids that were in the army at the same time went with us. When we arrived there was no one else we knew, except the old unit chaplain we called Padre. I guess he had been chaplain for the whole regiment during the war. He has been with us through it all. He was a nice man and had satisfied the religious needs of Jews, Catholics and Protestant soldiers. No one complained. I wondered why in peacetime there had to be such a big separation between these faiths. We used to get a Christmas card from the chaplain every year until a few years back, when his secretary sent the card and said he had passed away.

My old friend Snyder and his wife are still alive. He went back to Iowa and took over his Dad's Buick dealership. I had left him and his wife at Fort Lewis during training and later he had been on Okinawa. Kathleen and I went to Iowa in 1984 and visited him and his wife. It was really nice to see them again. We sent each other Christmas cards every year with a note in it. His card is the only one I get now.

I guess age has probably taken its toll on many. I still wonder what happened to Saki Joe. He was probably an alcoholic and you wouldn't want to be around him in peacetime. He'd taste anything in any bottle he found. On Leyte he was my second scout though, and solid as a rock. I knew he would always be there and I could count on him. Also, what happened to Pop? He was only thirty, but old to us. He must have been wounded on Okinawa. I remember he and I carrying down the soldier that had been hit by the Jap knee mortar. He was sayin', "Don't let me die, Pop," and he died.

I wish they would have had someone with combat experience go back and tell the new troops, the replacements, what we had learned. It would have saved so many lives. The old drill sergeants had made us hard, but they couldn't tell us about combat because they had never experienced it. I do remember one thing that I had heard all through training, and it seemed to be true in combat. Good soldiers get scared, but have no fear. Fear is what keeps them from doing their job when they get scared.

Portrait Of A Man
October 1993

It was a pleasant fall morning and Vernon had been watching the two rooster pheasants by the hickory tree for almost 30 minutes. For awhile it looked as if they were going to fight, but apparently they settled their differences. He hadn't shot a pheasant in quite a few years, and didn't intend to hunt or eat them any more. They were too much fun to watch. If you shot them one day, you couldn't watch them the next. It just kinda ended a pheasant's career, and Vernon didn't want to do that any more.

The day before a car had pulled into the driveway and a man stepped out dressed in hunting gear. "You know there are six big tough rooster pheasants setting in the edge of your cornfield?" "Yep, I know they're out there," Vernon replied. "Are you gonna hunt them?" "No I'm not gonna hunt them, and neither are you." That ended that conversation, and the man left.

Vernon still thought about the war, and some memories were vivid. Kwajalein hadn't lasted that long, but was one continuous four day and night battle because the Japs couldn't get away. Leyte was a long fight with little food, water and only one change of clothes in two and a half months. The rain and mud were terrible and they kept promising replacements after the next river, but none arrived. They said on Okinawa we would be relieved after the next hill, but we weren't until there weren't enough of us left to fight. Supposedly after 24 days there were only 32 men left out of the 199 in our company.

Vernon was 73 now, and there were things about the war that bothered him more now. He didn't go to church, but still believed in religion. If there was a heaven, and he made it there, he'd always heard that you'd meet all your friends and enemies. Would all those Japs be lined up waiting for him, and ask, "Why did you kill me? Why did you kill me?" It bothered him enough that he asked Kay what she thought, and Kay had said she didn't know and couldn't answer his question.

Along with Harvey and his wife Gert, they were invited to a neighbor's house for supper. The hostess was quite religious, and in the course of the evening Vernon again brought up the subject of heaven and whether or not the Japs would be there and ask why he had shot them. The lady simply replied that in wartime things were different. Vernon hadn't said anything, but he was thinking, "Have we got two books to go by? A bible for peacetime and another for war?" Something just didn't seem right to him that in wartime you could kill people you didn't like, but in peacetime you couldn't.

Another thing bothered him. On Leyte he thought he actually got to enjoying killing Japs too much. It was almost like hunting rabbits. As first scout he was good at it. He knew where and how they would be hiding. For awhile his unit was killing 20 to 30 a day. When one of his buddies got shot he wanted to kill 8 or 10 right now, just for payback. Once he had shot almost forty and in the process burned up his gun. That was real payback. Actually any time you shot a couple you were treated like you had hit a home run. The idea was to get them all killed so you could go home. There still had to be something wrong with liking to kill.

In basic training they were told gory stories about the way the Japs had treated American prisoners, and the hate began to build. If there was any question about killing Japs it was erased when he first saw the two dead Americans on Kwajalein. This was for keeps. Still, when there was time to think he wondered how complete strangers could hate enough to kill each other. Probably the Japs were told the same kind of stories about Americans. They must have thought we were going to torture them, for they wouldn't surrender. Over 56,000 Japs had been killed on Leyte. They died in the hills and no one knew who or where they were. They had mothers and fathers too.

He still didn't feel like he could ever be friendly with Japs, even after all these years. They had just killed too many of his friends. Maybe like water, some could turn the hate on when it was needed, and turn it off when it wasn't. That was hard for Vernon to accept.

Vernon limped back toward the house, relying heavily on the cane. One hip joint had been replaced, but the other caused a lot of pain now. If Kay hadn't been so sick this year he would have had that one operated on too. For a moment the distraction of the pain was interrupted by a moment of satisfaction. The tall brick farmhouse and the neat yard reminded him of the hard work he and Kay had put into this place, and how proud he was of it, and his family.

He hesitated again, when a pheasant cackled in the distance. A slight smile creased his face. "It's a good thing Jake's not here big rooster, or you wouldn't be that brave."

JUST MARRIED KATHLEEN AND VERNON   AUGUST 2, 1947

My best hired hand

Soldier Boy home

Brand new, and mine!

Mother and Dad's Fortieth Anniversary.   Back row left Robert, Harvey, Vernon, Mildred and
Katherine.
Below: Vernon with Carol, Garald and Jayne.

Vernon Heppe at home on Peterson Road, Ionia, MI. 1993.